HOW TO LAUNCH
YOUR PRIVATE INVESTIGATION BUSINESS:
90 DAYS TO LIFT OFF!

John A Hoda
CLI, CFE

How to Launch your Private Investigation Business: 90 Days to Lift Off!

Copyright John A. Hoda (2019)

All rights reserved. No part of this publication may be reproduced, stored in a retrieval system, or transmitted in any form or by any means with the prior written permission of the publisher.

ISBN: 978-0-9890201-4-5

Requests to publish work from this book should be sent to john@johnhoda.com.

Cover and Interior Illustrations, Titling, and Interior Layout: Creative Jay (creativejay.com)

HOW TO LAUNCH YOUR PRIVATE INVESTIGATION BUSINESS

90 DAYS TO LIFT OFF!

John A Hoda
CLI, CFE

INTRODUCTION

JOHN A. HODA

This book is written by a person who considered himself an investigator first and a business person second. It took a long time to blend those roles seamlessly to run a successful private investigation business. Understand that being a great investigator doesn't guarantee you will have a tremendous private investigation business. Some will argue that your investigative mindset may get in the way of your operational skills and your business creativity. There is an axiom that says the great bricklayer with average business skills will make less money than the average bricklayer with excellent business skills. You may be able to find anyone but to help anyone see you, you must think like a marketer.

I am not an MBA or a business coach with a good grasp of generic business principles, applying a multipurpose plan to a private investigations business no differently than to a pest control company or a pizza restaurant. I am speaking as a private investigator to private investigators. My goal is to help you avoid the minefields and chart a course for greater success. I know where the mines are hidden, just below the surface. I almost sailed into a few.

INTRODUCTION

The other thing to remember is that you are a professional, in most states, a licensed professional, and that you provide a service. The more your service is specialized, and the more unique your approach is, the less the consumer will view your services as a commodity. More money for you, and you stand above the herd.

As a working investigator, I know what it's like to have an investigator's mindset. I remember thinking like an investigator can sometimes get in the way of making business decisions as they relate to your time management and how you may want to approach new ventures. My experiences through the last twenty-one years have come from some hard-knock lessons and near disasters but, through it all, I was able to forge ahead and have stayed profitable for 84-plus quarters. I've been able to meet all of my financial obligations and have created a retirement plan that will allow me to retire at a date earlier than I had initially projected.

Before we get much further into the introduction, I want to share a personal anecdote with you—one of many to come but let me start with this one.

A few months ago, I was riding with a friend. He was a long-time private investigator and had many years under his belt before I even started back in 1997.

He asked me, "John if you had to do it all over again, would you do it?"

I surprised him with my answer. I told him, knowing what I know now, I would not have leaped. That caused him to raise an eyebrow. I said to him that at the time I decided to go in business for myself, I had a very comfortable position as a well-respected senior special investigator for a significant property & casualty insurance company and was being interviewed for management positions at other special investigations units. I had a very steep mortgage and was paying for both daycares and saving for college education for my two children. My wife had a good job, a steady income, and excellent benefits. After a financial scare nine years earlier, we had set aside six months of gross income, so there was somewhat of a cushion; however, the income that I would have to replace from my job with my new venture was quite a bit. I would have to make that up within seven or eight months of the start-up, or I would have to bail out.

I told my long-time friend that I did not fully appreciate the risk I was about to undertake. I had excellent investigative skills. I was at the top of my game and was hoping to ply my trade doing precisely the same type of work as a private investigator instead of as a salaried employee. That didn't mean I had the business acumen to be able to run a business effectively. I didn't know how to market, and I thought cash flow was what you had in the checkbook at the end of the month. However, I did tell my friend that, having made that leap over twenty-one years ago and having succeeded through all these years, I have very few regrets.

Not only was I able to work in the area of my expertise, insurance fraud investigations, but I was also able to learn how to conduct investigations in the field of forensic genealogy and missing heir research. I also learned how to transfer my criminal investigative skills to that of a criminal defense investigator.

More importantly, I think this is the best part, and I was able to train investigators in my techniques and in the way I went about my investigations. Watching them apply those investigative skill sets to their cases was most gratifying, but more importantly, how they blossomed as investigators.

Does this story surprise you? I hope that, during the course of this book and this series, I will continue to surprise you and challenge some of your assumptions and beliefs. I hope to help you understand why some things are more comfortable than they seem and why some things are harder than they appear.

INTRODUCTION

Primarily, you'll learn which is which, without having to spend much time, money, and effort.

In a nutshell, I want to tell you about all those things I didn't know then and that I had to learn the hard way. These lessons are what I want to share with you here. I want to make your path a little easier and a little straighter, so you can get to your goals quicker and with less anxiety, make more money in your business and, at the same time, enjoy the work you love.

It would be unfair to try to have everyone fit into my mold of how I did things. That's why I've created three characters whom you can compare and contrast. Hopefully, you can learn from these different characters as they approach their liftoff.

First, I will introduce you to **Tony Russo**. He is about to retire from the New York City Police Department as a Detective Sergeant. He's looking to go into PI business where he'll work mostly in Queens, New York, and eastern Long Island.

Beth Clark is a two-tour veteran of the United States Army, with experience in Intelligence from her days in the sandbox of Afghanistan. She relocated to Austin, Texas. A single woman of color, looking to use her smarts and skills and to go into business for herself. She wants to see what she can do without having to deal with the layers of management or bureaucracy between her and the customer. She wants to build a business that will eventually run without her in its daily operations.

Finally, there is **my personal story** of getting prepared for my September 1997 launch date where I was looking to create a business to serve property & casualty insurance companies. My goal was to sell my business to my employees and retire wealthy and early.

We will explore the paths being taken by Tony, looking to work with professionals, Beth, looking to work with the consumers, and John, looking to leverage his specialized skills with specific businesses that would require them.

After I introduce you more fully to Tony, Beth, and John, we will look ahead to the book's sections and then, dive into the hard questions.

Trust me; you'll be glad I asked these hard questions in the beginning. I intend to save you time effort and money with the questions, exercises, and checklists.

INTRODUCTION

Tony Russo is about ready to pull the pin, as they say in police work. He's been on the job for twenty-seven years and is tired of all the bureaucracy and having to supervise a group of detectives who seem to be less interested in the profession than the benefits. He's itching to get out and work some cases on his own again and to simplify his life. This PI business for him is a lifestyle choice. He is looking to augment his pension and work on cases that interest him.

He has decided he wants to work with lawyers, accountants, and small business owners in the borough of Queens in New York City and possibly expand into neighboring Nassau County on Long Island. Combined, both have a population base of over two million people. It would certainly give him enough opportunities to do what he wants in a somewhat condensed geographic area.

Beth Clark is formerly from the Twin Cities of Minneapolis and St. Paul, Minnesota. Upon graduation from high school, she enlisted in the Army and served two tours in Afghanistan as part of an Intelligence unit. Beth is smart and ambitious. Now living in Austin, Texas, she's looking to start her business in that city providing services for regular people. Her business model is business-to-consumer or B2C. She does not have any role models for creating a company and is looking to start from scratch. She is presently working for an armed guard security service that allows her to schedule herself to work available hours while she methodically launches her business.

INTRODUCTION

John is 43 years old. He has been a police officer and has worked his way up in the insurance business to become a claims manager. He also was a Special Agent and Area Supervisor for the Insurance Crime Prevention Institute, providing fraud investigation services to the property and casualty insurance industry. Before launching his business, he was a senior special investigator and quality control SIU manager for different insurance companies. It is the year 1997, at the dawn of the internet. John has a young family and is looking to go out on his own. He wants to scratch the entrepreneurial itch and thinks his investigative methods can be replicated. He wants to grow a regional private investigations company providing insurance fraud investigation and complex investigations for property & casualty insurance companies in a territory from Bangor, Maine to Baltimore, Maryland.

DISCLAIMER
PLEASE READ

I have done my best to give you useful and accurate information in this book, but I cannot guarantee that the information is correct or will be appropriate for your particular situation. Law, procedures, and regulations change frequently and are subject to differing interpretations. It is your responsibility to verify all the information and the laws discussed in this book before relying on them. Noting in this book can substitute for legal advice and cannot be considered as making it unnecessary to obtain such advice. In all situations involving local, state and federal law, especially as it relates to PI regulations and carrying weapons, receive specific information from the appropriate government agency.

OVERVIEW OF THIS BOOK

WHAT TO EXPECT

Section One: Red Light / Green Light (Page 17)

We will talk about:

- The most common reasons for failure and the most common reasons for success and the impact of state licensing on your decision.

- How you're going to talk with your significant others or persons of influence to get buy-in on your decision.

- How to start thinking about beginning your business with the end in mind.

Section One ends with ten fundamental red light/green light questions that will help you determine whether or not you should even go further into the process of expending time and capital to build your business.

Section Two: How Not To Get Poor (Page 39)

We will talk about:

- How not to get poor in your business venture.
- How not to drive yourself into a severe debt or worse, bankruptcy.
- How to understand your full list of expenses and see what your true debts are.
- How to determine, in everyday layman's terms, what your savings and equity are.
- Calculating expenses for Tony, Beth, and John
- How to create your chart of monthly expenses

Section Three: Balance Sheets (Page 49)

We will talk about:

- Income, and the difference between income and revenue.
- Bookkeeping best practices.
- Remaining mindful of what your business is about.
- The impact of taxes, and implication of taxes, on your business.
- Creating a spreadsheet of expenses for Tony, Beth, John, and yourself.
- What revenue you need to break even after covering your business and personal expenses.

Section Four: Forget Mission, Vision, and Value Statements (Page 65)

We will talk about:

- Simon Sinek's TEDx talk on Why, How and What (18 minute YouTube video).
- Charting a Why, How, and What exercise for Tony, Beth, John, and yourself.

Section Five: Needs Analysis (Page 75)

We will talk about:

- Your customer's needs and how to meet those needs with existing or newly learned skill sets.
- Understanding the difference between the user and your ultimate buyer.
- Deciding what business you will be in B2B, P2P, B2C, or a hybrid.
- Who the target audience for Tony, Beth and John are, and determine your own target audience.
- John's story of the International Missing Heir Finders as an example of the above.
- Determining how much to charge per hour.
- Calculating your critical number, which is the most important number to track regularly.

Section Six: What's In A Name (Page 91)

We will talk about

- Naming your business
- Domain names
- Website hosting services

OVERVIEW OF THIS BOOK

- WordPress platform and themes
- Home page
- About page
- Services page
- FAQ page
- Maximizing your SEO for your target audience
- Email capture
- e-Commerce
- Sales Funnels
- Autoresponders
- Checklist

Section Seven: Marketing For The Investigator (Page 107)

We will talk about:

- How to get into the flow of marketing
- Generating Leads
- Qualifying your prospects
- Offering assurances
- Clarifying their questions
- Overcoming objections
- Getting the assignments
- Agreeing on price
- Up-sell strategies
- The importance of communicating with your client
- Testimonials or Customer Satisfaction Surveys
- Referrals
- Creating a one-page marketing plan

Section Eight: The Business Of Your Business (Page 127)
We will talk about:

- Business entities: sole proprietorship, a single member LLC, or an S or C Corporation
- Licensing, Bonding, and Insurance
- Methods to use to maintain your assignments
- Assignment logs
- Client reporting
- CRM or customer relationship management software
- Time management methods
- Accounting software
- Using a checklist during your 90 days to lift off

Section Nine: Countdown Summary (Page 145)
We will talk about:

- Putting all the pieces together in the building block fashion
- Tony's Sample plan
- Beth's Sample Plan
- John's Sample Plan
- The tasks that need to be done and where to put them on the launch schedule.

Section Ten: Bonus Story (Page 163)

- John's launch of Elm City Detectives, 9-21-12 to 1-1-13

SECTION ONE:
RED LIGHT / GREEN LIGHT

(you will thank me later)

SOBERING STATISTICS

What is the real cost of failure? One of my mentors Jimmie Mesis, the former owner and editor of *PI Magazine*, once told me 85% of all private investigators do not renew their licenses after two years. That is an astounding failure rate.

Similarly, statistics from the Small Business Administration say that after five years, 85% of all small businesses fail. Additionally, in the next five years, of those remaining 15%, another 85% of those businesses fail. So essentially, after ten years, only 3% of small businesses will still be in business.

I'm sure the statistics for private investigation businesses are very similar. You have to ask yourself why.

We will get into those reasons in a few minutes, but for now, let's talk about the real cost of failure. Let's talk about crushed dreams, lost capital, drained bank accounts, maxed out credit cards. Worse, how about those who took out a second mortgage and then had to file for bankruptcy?

SECTION ONE: RED LIGHT / GREEN LIGHT

Then there's the emotional factor of having to reenter the job force and explain to a prospective employer where you were for the last year or year and a half?

What about having to take calls from the aggressive collection agencies or angry creditors; people who trusted you enough to do business with you? All this has an emotional toll on your psyche.

How could this have been avoided? How could you have changed things? What could you have done differently? These are all questions that could go through your mind.

In a book titled *How To Launch Your Private Investigation Business: 90 Days To Lift Off*, you're wondering why the first section has to do with sobering statistics of failure. Well, it's because we've all seen lots of grainy television footage and movie footage of rocket ships that exploded on liftoff or while still in our atmosphere. A few of these, unfortunately, were human-crewed spaceflights.

The reality is that many rocket ship failures occur before rocket ships are launched successfully. There is a learning-from-failure principle here that the scientists gain knowledge from. My hope is you can build a business by learning from my failures and those of others, so you can avoid the hardship of becoming one of those failure statistics.

Most Common Reasons For Failure:

- You didn't want to be in business for yourself, and you're more comfortable working for someone else.
- Running out of money.
- Lack of paying customers.
- Not having a clear business plan (round peg - square hole)
- Not bothering to work the plan you made
- Squandering your time
- Chasing "bright shiny objects' or in other words, changing direction without a solid business case or reason to do so
- Not spending enough money on the proper equipment.
- Not allocating enough money for marketing (at least 10% of your expense budget)
- Biggest cause: not spending enough time on marketing your business.

Traits For Success:

- Burning desire to overcome all obstacles
- Positive attitude when dealing with problematic circumstances or people
- Preserving cash and understanding that "cash is king."
- Executing your game plan on a quarterly, monthly, weekly, and daily basis
- Understanding what the most important numbers for your business success are
- Exceeding customer expectations; Are you a problem solver?
- Consistently tweaking your plan to attract prospects and convert them into customers in a replicable and scalable manner
- Streamlined processes for the delivery of products or services to your clients
- Seamless integration of back-office processes that allow for the delivery of all products or services in an efficient manner

State Licensing–Do Not Pass Go If...

In a cursory check of state licensing requirements—and I am no expert, I expect you to check very carefully what your state requires in order to have a license—we see several states do not require any licenses such as Idaho and South Dakota.

Some states require licensing in towns if you wish to work in a particular city.

Then there is the question of what are the *requirements* to become licensed. They go from Alaska having no requirements, to Delaware having to have five years of investigative experience. In Arkansas, there is a need of two years of working with a PI in either Arkansas, Tennessee, Oklahoma, or Louisiana, and then passing an exam.

Some states require a college education; most don't, however, and you can substitute years of experience by having either an Associate's degree, Bachelor's degree, or even a Master's degree.

Some states require passing an examination (Nevada, Montana, and New York) and attending a 40-hour class (Louisiana).

This is a cursory review and is by no means advice on whether or not your state has a license requirement that you must meet.

Generally speaking, people come into the private investigation business from law enforcement, where their years of education and investigative experience qualifies them to apply for a license.

Other persons come into the investigative business by working for a private investigator or private investigations firm, from an apprentice role to a full-time employee status that allows them to secure their license.

The application process sometimes requires a background check, such as credit reports, driver histories, criminal checks, and fingerprinting which are all geared to protect the consumer from unscrupulous business practices.

SECTION ONE: RED LIGHT / GREEN LIGHT

A few states allow reciprocity between states and you should check the reciprocity agreements between states before thinking about crossing state lines.

I needed to secure a state license in New York, New Jersey, Connecticut, Massachusetts, Vermont, New Hampshire, and Maine, and town licensing in Rhode Island.

In the Commonwealth of Pennsylvania, you have to go before a county judge to be granted a license.

Almost all states require bonding; that is a performance bond. A performance bond is a *surety* bond and offers some compensation to aggrieved clients who have not received the services rendered. They can claim your bond.

Most states also require errors and omissions coverage. My state, Connecticut, requires a one-million-dollar policy and I have a two-million-dollar aggregate.

Some states also require a professional liability insurance.

Carrying a gun has its own rules and regulations. If you wish to carry a concealed weapon as a private investigator, you have to know your private investigator's code inside and out before even considering it. Understand a concealed carry license will increase your premium for your liability insurance and failing to disclose that you carry a gun as a regular part of your business would be grounds for your insurance company to deny coverage in the event your gun is involved in a claim being made against you.

Part of your homework, at this time, is to understand all the licensing requirements for the states where you wish to work, and whether bonding and insurance are required. You must especially understand the laws governing the carrying of the weapons or concealed weapons.

Personal Experience On Deciding To Take The Plunge

Back in 1996 and 1997, John had a young family and a steep mortgage. He and his wife were both paying for daycare and setting aside money for college for their two children, at the same time as funding their retirement accounts. They had created a budget for their combined expense. They were both in their early earning years when raises and promotions were regularly occurring. They were able to keep up on the necessary costs and had some money to go on occasional travel vacations.

Shortly after moving to Connecticut on a job promotion, the then-Governor instituted a personal income tax where there had not been one before. For the next two years, his family did not go on any vacations because the money that had been earmarked for vacations had to pay for the newly created personal income taxes. Thank you, Lowell Weicker.

When he began talking about going out on his own, his wife astutely pointed out that there was no one in his immediate family, and no one in her immediate family, who had any experience running a successful solo business, and neither of them had the business acumen to do so. She was also concerned about the loss of income during the time it would take to build the business up to where it would become profitable. These were very valid concerns, and those concerns were voiced both logically and emotionally. He spent much time, during the planning stages before liftoff, to assuage her fears he would be able to not only return his family to its standard of living but also would increase it.

It is at this time you have to think about having "the talk" with your loved ones and significant others about the changes self-employment will have on the family dynamic. You might have gone to a job location every day, and now you'll be working at home. Even working at home has its issues, as it relates to your workspace, time management, and how you're going to go about your business when house chores are calling.

Will you need to tighten the belt and explain to your family they may have to forgo some of their extravagances during the time it takes to ramp up your business? Are they willing to sacrifice financially now for the long-term benefit?

These are all questions to ponder at this time for one fundamental reason: you need to have allies during this significant time. It can be a very lonely time, especially in the private investigation business, to go out on your own. You will strive to launch a business by pitching prospects for the investigative services you wish to provide them. You will be met with your self-doubt when some prospects turn you down.

It is an uphill battle to try to launch a business without having the support of family and your closest friends. So, keep this in the back of your mind as you go through the next couple sections. Right now, it's okay to talk about the idea of wanting to go out on your own, but you need to have a little bit more understanding of the complexity of that decision before you talk with any family members or friends about doing so.

Begin With The End In Mind

This is one of the most important pieces of advice I wish I had received when I started out. Generally, I had an idea that I wanted to create a business I would be able to sell to my employees once we reached our goal of becoming a regional investigations firm covering the mid-Atlantic and New England states.

I didn't plan on having to learn the skill sets necessary to accomplish that goal. I thought my small team project management skills were sufficient. I was viewing the business through the eyes of an investigator and not through the lens of a business person. I failed to consider all the steps necessary to create a vibrant business that could operate competitively in ten mid-Atlantic and New England states. In the twenty-one years of self-employment, I observed other Private Investigators also fail to begin with the end in mind of what they hoped to accomplish and how did they foresee their business reaching its final stages.

For some, they just want to work for X number of years, then tell their clients that they're going to stop taking on new cases. When they reached their last case, they would turn off the lights and close the door behind them.

For others, it is creating a partnership and selling their share to the remaining partners as a part of a buyout.

A few want to eventually sell the business to a buyer with generous upfront terms or, more effectively, selling the company over time to their employees, which would give them a guaranteed income on a gradual buyout (more of that later in the series).

You have to begin with the end in mind, and you have to see the arc of your business clearly and where it's going to be at various stages in your life. The skills you have now may not be the skills you will need later to accomplish your end goal. Please keep this in mind as we proceed.

SECTION ONE: RED LIGHT / GREEN LIGHT

Abort! Abort! Abort!

Now it is time for a difficult discussion. I'm talking about what to do when things don't work out the way you thought they would.

Were there circumstances beyond your control, or circumstances that you didn't even contemplate, which sabotaged your launch? You have to outline specific criteria that will mean it's time to pull the plug. You must pick a date by which, if you are not making X dollars a week or month, regularly, you need to abort the mission. You need to know that it is much better to amputate the limb than bleed out and lose the body.

I knew too many people in the private investigation business that put a second mortgage on their house, maxed out their credit cards, and began robbing Peter to pay Paul to keep a leaky boat afloat. They would have been better off getting into the lifeboats and scuttling the ship. They would still have some money, some creditworthiness, and the ability to move back into the industry, without leaving much flotsam in the water.

I repeat it here: a serious discussion has to be held as part of "the talk" with the people important to you. Explain to them that, if by date certain, you have not reached X for your revenue, then the **exit plan** has to be activated.

So, as part of beginning with the end in mind, you need to know how you want your business to prosper—define what success looks like for you—and have an exit strategy, should various factors force you to abandon your self-employment goals for now.

Plan B: The Pivot

Besides ending your business on a profitable note or aborting it to retain what little capital you have left and returning to the workforce, the third option is called Plan B.

In the latest Silicon Valley start-up parlance, it is called a pivot. That is when you realize the direction in which you first sought to generate leads, prospects, and customers were faulty and, with your time and remaining resources, begin searching for different customers and/or customer acquisition methods to scale and replicate.

You might be still going after the same customer base but doing so in a different fashion, emphasizing a different skill set in meeting their needs or learning a new skill.

The pivot happens when you start listening to customers' wants and needs and pivot from what you *thought* they wanted.

RED LIGHT / GREEN LIGHT CHECKLIST

Ten Yes / No Questions

1. Do you have a burning desire?
2. Are you willing to work significantly longer hours than at present? Only a lifestyle business in retirement is the exception here.
3. Are you willing to work on some of the more mundane tasks of running a business consistently?
4. Are you willing to learn enough about bookkeeping, accounting, marketing, and sales to keep your fanny out of the fire?
5. If your business model requires you to be available for your customers on nights, weekends, or holidays, will you able to answer the bell as often as needed?
6. Are you or your family willing to tighten the belt during lean times or periods of protracted low cash flow?
7. Are you willing to learn new investigative skill sets to round out your services to your customers or clients?
8. Are you optimistic you will have the support of family and friends to launch your private investigation business?

SECTION ONE: RED LIGHT / GREEN LIGHT

9. Do you think you have sufficient capital to be able to afford your launch?
10. Have you successfully overcome adversity in the past?

> This checklist should be reviewed now and looked at again later if you decide to go on. It would help if you revisited this checklist when you have a better grasp on what it is you're going to do, how you're going to do it, and the money you're going to need to keep your business above water. Keep in mind; this checklist is predicated on the fact you will be capable of procuring the license in the states you wish to operate in.

Tony had to access his feelings. It was not always easy for a thinking man's detective at the NYPD. Cops and detectives have a way of burying feelings as they face the daily onslaught of murder, mayhem, and utter disregard for human life and private property. He had not thought about these red light/green light questions. He had seen a few of his colleagues go out on their own. Most ended up pulling private security details when they came up. Some made up bull when the going got tough and quit before heading to Myrtle Beach or Florida to play golf and take it easy.

Was he burned out? Would he pack it in when the going got tough? No, he wanted to get out from under the NYPD's rules and bureaucracy and work on his own. He missed working the street and wanted to pick and choose his caseload. Nothing else was fatal here. With his pension assured and with his wife's salary and backing, he didn't see any other show-stoppers. He could do this on his terms and at his own pace.

SECTION ONE: RED LIGHT / GREEN LIGHT

The red light/green light questions for Beth weren't even a speed bump on her road to launch. Years of taking orders in the Army and mining someone else's gold in the armed guard security business had her chomping at the bit. Yes, she needed to learn about business, but she would attack that like a six-miler through the rolling hills of Austin as the sun was rising. One thing the Army taught her in Afghanistan is that things change, and she had to always be on the look-out. Mistakes could get good people killed. She had a knack for breaking complex problems down into digestible parts even when the intel was sketchy. She had stayed friendly with some Army buds on Facebook and made some friends in Austin, and they were all gung-ho for her.

She knew she had to bootstrap this puppy from scratch. It had to be a soft launch.

CONGRATULATIONS!

After completing this checklist, you've decided to either move forward or to shelve your plans to launch your private investigation business.

I'm saying congratulations to the reader that decides to shelve their plans. By taking a few minutes now on the front end to do a gut check, you are saving yourself a lot of heartache, trouble, and expense later on, when one or more of these reasons could become the cause for your business failure.

For those readers wishing to go forward, again, congratulations! You've taken the time necessary to think about the business of your business, and this is going to become much more critical as you go forward.

"The first rule of entrepreneurship is not how to get rich. It's how not to get poor."

—Cliff Ennico, Attorney-at-Law

SECTION TWO: HOW NOT TO GET POOR

YOUR EXPENSES

In this section, we are going to talk about your expenses, your taxes, and what you have set aside for savings and equity. Don't be scared off by the word equity. After you make your last car payment, what is your car worth if you put a sales sign on it? If you had to sell your home right now, after expenses and paying off your mortgage note, what do you have left over? That is equity.

Do you really know your expenses?

A quick review of your checkbook register and credit card statement is not enough to know all of your expenses. You need to sit down and look at least twelve months and make a spreadsheet of the usual and recurring expenses. This will help you with the exercise below.

You will also have to think about what you'd be paying for health insurance, not just what is being deducted from your paycheck. What are all your other payroll deductions that, if you were to leave your employer, you would have to pay for yourself? If you think about it, each of your expenses is what goes out of your pocket after payroll deductions and taxes

What do you have left at the end of the month? Some people are in a negative cash position. They are not able to live on their paycheck and have to rely on paying exorbitant interest rates on larger and larger credit card balances. They keep kicking the can down the road. Eventually, the credit cards will have to be paid off.

How much debt are you carrying?

Mortgage? Car Loans? Furniture? Home Equity Line? Credit cards? Recreational vehicles? Timeshares? Tax repayments?

What are your savings and equity?

Savings are all monies you have set aside, separate from your operating accounts. I'm a little hesitant to call certificates of deposits or CDs 'savings' because of their lack of liquidity, in that you're not able to get your hands on that money right away (although you may be able to take a cash loan against the certificate of deposit at a hefty fee). You think of savings as your retirement accounts. Again, there are penalties for early withdrawal and tax consequences. Also, consider all your stocks and bonds and other financial instruments which can be converted to cash relatively quickly.

I think in terms of liquidity, with savings, as any financial instrument you can turn readily to cash within a short period.

Examples:

Tony, Beth, and John are looking to start their businesses within 90 days. They are looking at their expenses to see how much money they must earn to cover their necessary living expenses.

Keep in mind; this doesn't include what will be their one-time or short-term business expenses related to the formation and operating of their businesses.

Lastly, do not forget the tax consequence of their earnings and how much money they have to set aside for federal, state, and local taxes. Pay stubs will give you a ballpark idea, **but you should consult with an accountant about your set apart for your quarterly estimates.**

Expenses	Tony	Beth	John*	You
Mortgage/Rent	$1,750	$1,150	$1,475	
Car Expenses	$900	$275	$600	
Health Care/Co-Pays/Deductibles	$600	$620	$200	
Child Care/College Savings	$0	$0	$1,100	
Clothing	$100	$20	$75	
Food	$1,000	$400	$600	
Entertainment	$500	$154	$200	
Utilities	$325	$200	$300	
Loans	$500	$750	$0	
Credit Cards	$2,254	$500	$775	
Telephone	$54	$100	$300	
Household Repairs and Maintenance	$200	$20	$300	
Gym	$0	$20	$300	
Vacation	$200	$100	$200	
Gifts	$200	$34	$200	
Retirement Accounts	$200	$200	$200	
Total	$8,783	$4,502	$6,579	

*John's startup was in 1997, so for purposes of this writing, the numbers are inflated to equal values at the time of publishing.

SUMMARY

These expense items are not a totality of possible expenses you may be facing. They don't take into account such things as elder care, one-time expenses, emergencies, and so on. This exercise is to get you thinking of what your family unit's real spending is.

"Ouch," Tony thinks. "That hurt."

He and Mary had been living the good life. Even though she was an excellent cook and baker, they spent a ton of money eating out. They spared no expense on their vacations. "Need it? Put it on the credit card." "Want it? Put it on the credit card."

As their property value rebounded following the '08-'09 housing collapse, they remortgaged their house and cleaned up all of their credit card balances, only to let that insidious debt creep up again. He and Mary stared at the spreadsheet in disbelief, then in resignation. How did two smart, hard-working people allow this to happen *twice*?

Now he has to work and make more money than to replace his income. He has to get the credit cards paid off if they want to have any equity in the house they bought years ago and should have paid off by now.

He and Mary agree to cut back on the restaurants and upscale vacations. The car leases were lavish. Today's cars can last ten years, at the rate they put mileage on them. All across the board, the couple decides to tighten their belts and make the adjustments needed to spend less than they earn. Financial freedom becomes a new mantra.

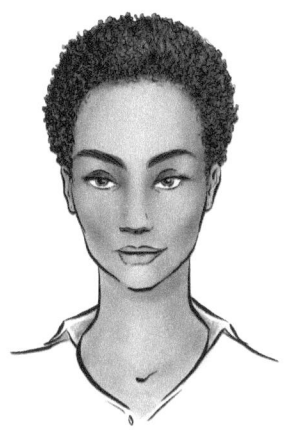

Looking at the numbers, Beth has two choices: Take on a second job or invest in her business and continue to float her debt until she can get into a positive cash-flow.

Co-signing the loans for a family member had been a mistake. They stopped paying on them, leaving her to face that nut every month now, and for the next three years. It was already refinanced down to the lowest interest rate she could get.

She is paying an average rent for a nice unit in a well-kept complex between the airport and downtown Austin. After years of living in spartan Army barracks, this is her only "extra."

Otherwise, she keeps a tight ship. Or so she thinks until she sees her spending on Starbucks and the independent coffee houses in the area. She lives on caffeine, and if she could hang a drip from the top of the Armored vehicles she rode in, she would. Those lattes and artisan drinks make up a whopping $210 a month.

The next day, after swallowing her nitro-infused cold brew, she buys a plain-vanilla drip coffee-maker and a hefty thermos. That saved money can go into the business.

SECTION THREE: BALANCE SHEET?

YOU DON'T NEED NO STINKING BALANCE SHEET.

BALANCE SHEET ACCOUNTS

The balance sheet has the simple but maddening equation:

Assets = Liabilities + Equity

Try to understand what your accountant is saying when he does a trial balance at the end of the year. Thank him for explaining it to you again. Nod your head enthusiastically and say, "Wow!"

I found that the most essential items to be watching are on your income statement or what is called your profit and loss statement (P&L). Later on, I will give you a Cash Flow Snapshot that you calculate on the 15th and the 30th of every month.

Mostly, if you run out of money, you either have to take out loans to pump up the business or factor your receivables or do something drastic to stay in business. So you have to concentrate less on the static Balance Sheet and more on the profit and loss statement along with the cash flow snapshot as a way of maintaining your fiscal health with your business. Your profit and loss statement is made up of income items and expense items that are a little bit more simpler to understand.

Knowing some basics of bookkeeping include the need to discuss debits and credits, knowing what accounts can be debited and credited and why and how what journal entries are made to your general ledger. These are all words that you may not be familiar with, but in concise order, you'll have to get a general idea of what they all mean to understand the basics of running a business.

Bookkeeping Tips
The Internet has made it so much easier to find information on any topic—at least for learning its nomenclature. Go to YouTube and search for 'basic bookkeeping' or 'basic accounting,' and you'll see some paid advertising that will give short tutorials explaining the basics. The most important decision you're going to make, as it relates to how to keep your records, is whether or not you'll use an accountant and a bookkeeper or some combination thereof.

I do not recommend doing your own accounting. My experience is that you should have a professional, preferably a certified public accountant (CPA), look over your books. At tax time, you don't want to be David without his slingshot standing up against the Goliath of your Federal Government (IRS) or your State's Department of Revenue Services.

Most importantly you want to separate your deposits and the check writing functions and keep them away from either your accountant and your bookkeeper. I would recommend in the first years, you handle the checkbook yourself and either make the electronic payments or write out the checks yourself. Delegate

> the separation of the bookkeeping from the bill paying so that no one person has complete control over your checkbook other than yourself.

We will talk about the way to choose an accountant later in this book; however, the critical point to know when you are choosing an accountant is what the accountant's preferred method of keeping your books will be.

The big daddy of accounting software is QuickBooks by Intuit, and there are other outstanding and less expensive computer software options to ease and facilitate entering all your information and handling online banking as it pertains to your business.

I use QuickBooks because my accountant uses QuickBooks. I also have firsthand knowledge of FreshBooks and Wave and can recommend either one of them. There are other, cheaper, options and yes, there's even a manual ledger system you can utilize if your business is small enough. As long as you keep your receipts and track all your payments and income, a paper system could work as effectively. However, when you want to compare one year to another or one quarter to a previous quarter, the electronic systems can provide reporting tools that make them a definite advantage over paper records.

I suggest you look at some of the tutorials on YouTube for whichever accounting and bookkeeping software you and your accountant decide to use, to familiarize yourself with their user interface.

Over the last four years, I've learned how to work as my own bookkeeper, but I also work with a Certified Public Accountant four times a year, to make sure my entries are not off the rails. I keep scrupulous paper copy records of all my transactions, so we can go back to the source document if I've created a problem or if I made a mistake.

SECTION THREE: BALANCE SHEET

I will repeat this often throughout the course of this book: you are in the business of private investigations. Whether it's running a pizza shop, pest control business, or private investigations company, certain universal things go into your books. How you make your bookkeeping entries, how you keep your books, what accounting method you utilize, what accounting software you use—these are all decisions universal to any business whether you're selling a product, goods, or services.

As a business person, I cannot stress enough the importance of understanding the primary language of bookkeeping and accounting to understand your business better.

Later on, we'll talk about how to set up your budget and how to compare that budget against your actuals. You'll be able to measure the growth or decline of your business on a monthly, quarterly, and yearly basis. You will also be able to compare said growth or decline against last year's numbers for the same periods.

You have to understand how these numbers are generated, so when you look at some outliers or variances, you will be able to deduce where they came from intelligently. Some figures look somewhat out of place because they are either too large or too small.

As a glaring example of understanding cash flow, imagine taking on a new client who promises you a ton of work. You ramp up your operation and hire new people. You spend time training and equipping them. You insure them and make sure the appropriate taxes are taken out for them with your payroll service. You make this new client a priority and stop marketing to other clients and possibly neglect your other steady clients. You do lots of work for the client and do a satisfactory job, maybe even an excellent job. You have paid out many expenses and payroll before you send them a large invoice. You can see where this is going.

Had you been watching the numbers, you would know how dangerous this is, because when this client decides not to pay, or that they want to negotiate your bill, what is your leverage? The work is done, and payroll is looming.

They are negotiating from a position of strength, and they could put you out of business because you failed to foresee the impact of that client's work on the overall health of your business.

Don't Forget Taxes, Ever!

As part of your business, you will be hopefully earning an income. With that income, you'll have income taxes. Depending on where you live, you may have both Federal and State income taxes. Some municipalities even have an additional income tax on top of that. Some states tax Private Detective services, so you have to make sure to keep track of your sales tax if you work in those jurisdictions. Then, you either pay them on a monthly or quarterly basis. In any event, you have to make sure to have enough money set aside to pay your taxes at the end of the year or, as I do, quarterly.

My accountant helps me determine how much money I made the previous year and we estimate how much money my business is going to make in the upcoming year, and he provides me with a breakdown as to what I have to pay quarterly to both the Feds and the State. So, as income comes in during the course of each month, I set aside money—I usually do so in a separate account—to pay the quarterly estimated income taxes and the monthly Sales Tax.

In December, my accountant comes in with me, and we look at the books and see how things are shaping up. He does a trial balance. We went over the books in July, so there should be no surprises there. He comes in again after the year closes and we sit down and finalize the books of the year. By doing so, he's able to give me an estimate of what I'm going to be paying for my taxes in the following year, and we set aside that amount. Now, if I'm doing much better than anticipated, I will spend much more in taxes and have to increase my set-asides. Conversely, if I am not doing as well as we planned, then I may be able to ease off the pedal a little bit on setting aside money for taxes.

The way I look at this is: if I've set aside more money in taxes than I needed to, I can either apply the overage to the first quarter of the following year, or I can supplement my IRA and even lower my taxes further for this year.

However, it is essential that you never forget taxes, I can't stress that enough. I recall in my second or third year of business, my first accountant had done my trial balance in the middle of December and said I set aside more than enough money for all my taxes and I could expect to receive a refund. On the day the taxes were due, he called me up to tell me that he had made a mistake in the calculation of my taxes and I had to come up with $4,500 by midnight. I utilized an interest-free credit card advance to meet the deficit. I then had to add a $400 monthly payment essentially to the following year's expenses, which made it more difficult to see an accurate profit and loss for the following year.

Needless to say, I fired that accountant, and I've been with the same accountant now for almost 20 years.

Business Expenses

Just as we performed an exercise on your personal expenses, now we are going to concentrate on business expenses to give you an idea of what costs to budget for your first year of business.

You need to understand what your expenses are for running this business, as well as what your personal costs are. You also have to remember to set aside money to cover your taxes as well.

Business Expenses	Tony	Beth	John	You
Subcontractors	$100	$200	$200	
Database Usage	$100	$200	$200	
Transcription	$0	$0	$0	
Insurance: Life, Health, Disability	$950	$1600	$1325	
Car: Payments, Gas, Insurance, Maintenance, Repairs	$995	$275	$675	
Computer & IT	$50	$450	$200	
Equipment	$100	$200	$100	
Payroll & Payroll Expenses	$0	$1,050	$1,100	
Professional Services, Accounting, Bookkeeping, etc.	$300	$300	$300	
Marketing	$200	$400	$300	
Travel & Meals	$100	$150	$125	
Meals & Entertainment	$50	$50	$50	
Bank Charges	$7.50	$12.50	$5.50	
Dues & Subscriptions	$25	$30	$30	
Miscellaneous	$20	$20	$20	
Office Expenses	$15	$20	$20	
Monthly Total	$3,015.50	$4,957.50	$4,650.00	
Yearly Total	$36,186.00	$59,490.00	$55,806.00	

This list of expenses is by no means complete. It doesn't include offices outside of the home or Internet costs. I would instead provide a representative sample than have your eyes glaze over with every possible expense related to your business. Some expenses were lumped into categories.

SECTION THREE: BALANCE SHEET

What are your annual expenses related to the running of your business? Tony, Beth, John, and you may each be in different areas of the country, doing different types of work, serving different types of customers, using different kinds of business models. As a result, your expenses may vary widely.

I tried to estimate what the monthly expenses for Beth would be in the business-to-consumer (B2C) world. She is also is younger and has no spouse to lean on for health benefits. On the other hand, she has a higher life premium and disability premium than Tony or John. Beth is relying more on Internet marketing and digital advertising and, as such, requires the services of an Internet-savvy technical person whose services fall under the IT category. Tony, Beth, and John can each deduct their actual mileage using their personal vehicles used for business travel, per IRS regulations.

There will be balance sheet adjustments made by your accountant as it relates to depreciation for your vehicle. You have to give an honest estimate as to how much of your vehicle you use for business use versus personal use (if you track your business mileage, divide that by your car's total mileage for the year). In Beth's case, she's going to buy a tricked-out van with tinted windows and, given the heat in Austin, Texas, install additional silent air conditioning. Because she only uses the van for her business use, it is entirely a business expense. Tony, on the other hand, is utilizing his personal vehicle for business which includes a bumper-to-bumper maintenance plan. He has a higher lease payment than both Beth and John.

Tony's professional to professional business requires half of the marketing expense that John does in the business-to-business and Beth spends more in the business to consumer business model than either one of them.

You have to see what your business model is and determine how much of marketing will be involved to generate leads for your business. If you don't have an idea how to put together this budget at present, I would gently suggest to you that for each line item, you add up Tony, Beth and John's expense then divide by three. Make that your line item expense, unless you know that there's a specific expense that is going to be greater or less based upon your existing equipment and situation. You can make the changes accordingly.

From the previous section, you see that Beth has a monthly personal expense of $4502. Add her business expense of $4,957.50, and **she needs at least $9,459.50 each month to break even after taxes.**

John's personal expenses are $6,579. When splitting that in half, because his spouse is responsible for half, his personal expense costs total $3,289.50. Add that to his business expenses of $4,650. To break even, **John has to earn at least $7,939.50 each month after taxes.**

In Tony's situation, we will assume his wife is responsible for 25% of their income, his pension is 25% of their income, and his business paying 50% of their remaining $8,783 personal expenses, leaving him $4,391.50 personal expenses added to his business expenses of $3,015.50. **Tony needs to make $7,407 to breakeven after taxes.**

> What is the amount of money that you have to make per month to break even?

At this point you might say to me, "John, how am I supposed to know what my business expenses might be given that there are other categories you didn't mention?"

I understand your concern. However, you have to start somewhere, and your projected budget is precisely that. You'll have to extrapolate from this information given to you by a veteran PI business owner telling you what his expenses are every month, annually amortized for any given year, and from the hypothetical expenses for two other investigators based upon their unique situations. It should give you a basis from which you can make a decision.

Of course, you might try to look at some of those expenses and see how you can do away with them, or how you can lower them. Bootstrapping your business is a beautiful way to get started. On the other hand, there might be some additional expenses that you or I did think about.

Over time, a pattern will emerge from your regular expenses as well as the occasional one-time expense which you can annualize; however, it's important to realize that by getting a hold of your personal expenses and making an honest projection of your business expenses, you'll have an idea of how much money you need to make after taxes.

Note: this would be a good time to revisit the red light green light checklist questions. You will thank me later.

Tony is breathing a little easier. He survived his fifteen-rounder with his personal expenses. Having a sharp pencil and a template to follow, he determined his life-style business was easier to maintain than other business models that are reliant on a robust website and employees. A spare bedroom, a good car, decent laptop, and the other necessities were less daunting to calculate than the bloated personal expenses he and his wife were supporting.

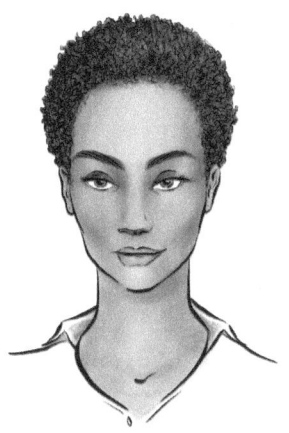

Staring at the numbers, Beth kept working them and working them. She knew that if she wanted to build a company where she would eventually move out of fulfillment and back-room operations, she had to build it from the ground up with that end in mind. Health benefits for her employees were poking her hard in the ribs. Going from the Army to an established company with generous benefits left her shaking her head. She was tri-athlete healthy, but she was also pragmatic. What if some joker was texting while driving by her on her bicycle? What if some of the chemicals she was exposed to back in the Sandbox were to manifest themselves in the form of cancer? She needed to have a rock-solid disability plan to go with her veterans insurance.

This was no place to cut corners. She struggled with how to set up her website. Luckily for her, she was invited out to tacos with some of the good folks at locally based AppSumo. One of their Austin-based 'Sumo-lings' agreed to work with her to build a world-class website. They were intrigued by her business model and wanted to apply their tools to a start-up PI business. These people had serious creds, and she knew not to trust this critical aspect of her marketing to somebody that could disappear with her passwords and hold her website hostage.

SECTION THREE: BALANCE SHEET

John went about bootstrapping his business slightly differently. He created an affiliation with a surveillance company that worked exclusively for insurance companies. He referred them his customers with surveillance while working their customers' investigative needs. John worked the weekends and holidays as a surveillance operative at above-average sub-contractor rates for most of 1997 to pay his one-time-only start-up costs. He had no debt on his Labor Day launch date.

BALANCE SHEET ACCOUNTS

SECTION FOUR: FORGET MISSION, VISION, AND VALUE STATEMENTS

LET'S TALK ABOUT YOUR WHY, HOW, AND WHAT

START WITH THE WHY...

YouTube search: **TedX Simon SINEK Start with the why...** It's 18 minutes long and worth the viewing. I'll be here waiting.

Bankers and lenders will tell you that you have to make a business plan and that you have to toil over a mission, vision, and values statement. They love to go to great lengths expounding upon the necessity for this. The statements are meant to give your company culture the proper grounding from which all decisions are made, from the CEO on down to the boiler-room service reps.

Of course, the latest Mission, Vision, and Value statements are brought in by the new CEO replacing the Mission, Vision, and Value statements of the previous CEO.

All the C suite executives go off to a retreat center, preferably in a very expensive and idyllic setting, where a high-priced facilitator guides them in team-building and trust-building exercises. It's comical to see the CEO fall backward into the arms of his COO, CIO, and CFO. Miraculously, they don't drop him. (That's the most heavy-lifting they have done in a while.)

SECTION FOUR: FORGET MISSION, VISION, AND VALUE STATEMENTS

At the end of the retreat, after word-smithing every word, every comma, phrase, sentence, and paragraph to death, they are excited to return to headquarters with a new vision and a mission, along with a value statement to clarify the most important values of the Corporation. Then, with much fanfare, it gets transmitted down to the Directors, then to the managerial staff, then down to the supervisory ranks, then finally to the line employees where the plaque covers a tear in the break room wallpaper next to the clock.

Needless to say, after several years of disappointing quarters, when the earnings and return on investment is less than what they would have earned in Treasury Bills, that CEO is let go with a buyout package of more money than you or I make in a lifetime, and a new team is assembled and the same process repeats.

As you can see, I am not exactly a big fan of the way mission, vision, and value statements are created in publicly held corporations. I certainly don't see the necessity of them for a business plan of a person looking to launch a private investigation business with one employee (themselves).

Having said that, I'm glad you had a chance to listen to and watch the straightforward message of Simon Sinek as he related to you **Why, How, and What.**

I can wax poetic and say the **Why** is your true North and is what you should be thinking about every morning when you start your business day.

The **How** and the **What** should be your work. Does your work align with your true North? Do the **How** and **What** provide a clear roadmap to your goals?

There are two reasons to talk about the **why, how, and what** in this section of the book after you've done the exercises regarding your true personal expenses and your estimated business expenses.

First, what are you passionate about and second, how will you generate revenue doing what you love? It is in this intersection where you begin to formulate your ideas on how to create revenue to be successful enough to be able to meet your expenses on a weekly, monthly and yearly basis.

Tony is looking to work professional to professional (P2P). He wants to target attorneys, certified public accountants, and property management firms for professional services, along with small to medium sizes businesses.

His **why** is to be on his own and out from underneath the entrenched bureaucracy of the NYPD so he can provide his clients who really care about the outcome with the **what**, i.e., the best possible investigation he can put together on their behalf.

His **how** is to execute all of the investigative objectives, based upon the best information made available to him and by expertly communicating his findings.

His **what** is combining the latest Internet and social media search tools with excellent interviewing skills and 27 years' worth of contacts to secure evidence and facts his clients will eventually use in court.

SECTION FOUR: FORGET MISSION, VISION, AND VALUE STATEMENTS

For Beth, who is looking to work in the business to consumer world (B2C), her **why** is to build a private investigations business she can eventually sell to a larger competitor, allowing her to adventure travel. She chafes after years of army life and now, working in a multi-layered Armed Guard company. She will escape to freedom by creating a replicable and scalable lead generation strategy to convert prospects into customers (**how**). These customers are individuals who suspect their significant other of infidelity.

Her **what** is doing surveillance, database searches, and social media searches.

John's **why**, how, and what has the benefit of hindsight. John's why was the need to validate his investigative methodology could be replicated, and a high level of expertise could be transmitted to motivated individuals.

How, he did that by rigorous recruiting, hiring, training, supervision, and evaluation methods he created. He was going to prove his concepts with his initial investigators, then replicate and scale those methods as the business expanded outside of Southern New England and New York.

The **what** would be providing high-end insurance fraud investigative services for special investigation units and insurance fraud, as well as complex investigations on behalf of property and casualty companies.

Now I'm sure there is a way to shoehorn these three different investigators' **why, how, and what** statements into a business plan with a mission, vision, and value statement; however, I think you would agree a thought-out why, how, and what statement is much more focused and serves as a better framework to help you make every business decision.

In John's case, the **why** became more obvious in retrospect when considering the amount of time and effort John put into creating his team of insurance fraud investigators, and how he replicated his training methods and sold the investigators on his methods.

It was also obvious in the way John supervised the investigators and reviewed their reporting. It was a great satisfaction to John to be able to create a cadre of investigators who performed at a high level daily and learned the time management skills to maintain a heavy caseload while doing so.

Think of the why, how, and what as both the emotional drivers for yourself as well as how you will meet the emotional needs of your clients with the work that you will perform and how well you will do it.

After you write out your why, how, and what, let it sit for a day or two, then ask yourself the question: Is this "Hell yeah"?

If not, revise it until you can say "Hell yeah!" If you can't, then this is gut check time.

> If your answer is not "Hell, yeah," do you really want to take on this risk of time, effort, and capital?
> How does your plan resonate with you, now that you've looked at your personal expenses and projected your business expenses? Is it still a "Hell, yeah"?

If so, now is the time to have 'the talk' with the people whose support you are counting on. You can verbalize **why** you want to take this risk, **how** you are going to provide services to your specific target audience with your skills and tools, and **what** their desired outcome will be. You will be able to show your breakeven analysis after intelligently calculating your personal and projected business expenses.

I personally find the **why, how, and what** exercise to be much more fulfilling and meaningful than trying to create a lofty mission, vision, and values statement. I also think that if you keep **why, how, and what** front and center, it will have more meaning to you as you go about planning your weekly and daily tasks. However, that's just my opinion.

SECTION FIVE:
NEEDS ANALYSIS

"GAPS"

YOU'RE FILLING GAPS

Sylvester Stallone's portrayal of Rocky in 1976—which won him the Academy Award for best picture—has a scene where he's talking to his future brother-in-law, Paulie.

> Paulie asks, "Hey, Rock, what do you see in my sister [Adrian]?"
> Rocky replied, "Gaps."
> "Gaps?"
> "Yeah, we fill gaps. She fills my gaps. I fill her gaps."

When you really think about it, you're providing a service for individuals or businesses. You're filling gaps. When you're in a private investigation business, you're filling the gap between what the client knows or suspects and what they need to know. Your job is all about meeting those needs of filling gaps.

SECTION FIVE: NEEDS ANALYSIS

Aligning Customer Needs With Your Skill Sets Or Learning New Ones

A criminal defense attorney has a client who insists he is innocent of any wrongdoing. How do you meet their needs? What investigation has to be undertaken to allow them to go into court and create reasonable doubt?

A wife suspects her husband of cheating and wants to get the proof of his infidelity.

A landlord has to locate a deadbeat renter that skipped out and owes thousands of dollars for back rent.

An insurance company suspects a policyholder of torching their car.

Each of the customers has different needs, and each investigation requires different skill sets.

As investigators firstly, we are sometimes hammers always looking for nails. That's how we find our customers and find our niches. However, as business people, is it better to chase the skill or the customer?

Look at Beth's situation as she builds a business with consumers on fidelity investigations. Her surveillance skills are easily transferable to workers compensation and disability insurance companies. The hammer is apparently searching for other nails, but the search takes her away from her preferred customer base. Her branding and website are for consumers, not businesses.

Instead, what if she learned new skills sets for her existing customer base? She is filling their other gaps. For example, she could invest the time to learn how to locate missing teens quickly for frantic parents when Law Enforcement gives them a cold shoulder. Does Beth want to take on a myriad of general investigations to be able to service her clientele more completely?

Would it be better for Beth to subcontract out some cases so far afield from her skill set, to keep the customer happy while taking a referral fee from the subcontractor?

I don't often recommend books for investigators; however, there is a section in *What Color Is Your Parachute?* by Richard Bolles. In it, he speaks eloquently on how skill sets can translate into other similar skills, or those that are very close, by comparison, that would be easy to bring to proficiency with a little effort.

In Tony, Beth and John's situation, all of their clients need to undertake asset checks on the person they are investigating. The reasons for each customer stem from a different business need, but the skill set is the same. If you don't know how to do asset checks, do you learn how to do them legally, in compliance with the Federal Credit Reporting Act and the Graham Leach Bliley Act?

Is it lucrative enough for you to learn how to create a scalable and repeatable process around asset checks that can give your clients the answers they seek?

If you choose not to learn the skills to meet this need, do you offer another solution for your client, or do you send them elsewhere on a referral? Don't tell me you will tell your customer you don't do that type of search and refuse to help them fill their need.

Another customer need could be that of an SIU investigator or a criminal defense attorney to do a background check on the subject of the investigation or the alleged victim.

Not to make your head spin anymore, but there's also the question of who is the buyer and who is the user? What the buyer wants and what the user needs are sometimes not the same. For example, the gap is seen usually between what the individual consumer thinks they need and what their lawyer has to bring to court in the form of facts or evidence.

Another example is the property and casualty insurance industry, where the buyer may be the highest echelon in the claims department, and the user is the claims adjustor with a sticky claim to deal with. The special investigation unit investigator or the claims adjuster would be the user of the investigation that you provide. However, the payer (buyer) for that investigation is their employer. How are the buyer's needs different from the user's needs, and how do you align them in your marketing and investigative processes?

The buyers', users', and attorneys' needs all have to be juggled by the investigator.

What Business Are You In?

Business-to-Business (B2B): User may not be the buyer. Multiple decision-makers in the process. Contracts, purchase orders, and retainers are usual. Budgets are set, and pricing is subject to volume discounting.

- Professional-to-Professional (P2P): I've not seen this phrase elsewhere, so I'm going to take ownership of it. You, as a licensed professional investigator, are reaching out to other professionals such as Attorneys, Property Managers, Certified Public Accountants, Certified Financial Planners, or anyone that has a professional designation as determined by their schooling and their licensing. They spell out the investigative objective for their clients. A retainer is taken if their client is the buyer and not them. Flat rate pricing for simple cases may replace the usual hourly arrangements.

- Business-to-Consumer (B2C): Think of when you, as a consumer, Google for goods or services to be rendered. You find businesses that will offer their goods or services. You go to their websites and get into their sales funnel to purchase a product or service. An individual walking can do the same in a retail establishment. As this applies to your business, the client is a private individual, and you're dealing with their personal checkbook. Their need affects them personally as opposed to a business decision being made. You are the business they are reaching out to. You could be a solo investigator, or you could have a team working with you. You could work with other associates, but the C part of the equation is more important. Your focus is all on the consumer, the private individual.

- Hybrid: For example, you are an expert. Anybody who needs your expertise comes to you. You market to the highest paying users/buyers. On the other end of the spectrum, you are the only guy or gal in a remote section of the state. You are the only game in that county. You market to other Private Investigators around the world to let them know you are the best solution in that zip code. Your website is optimized for people to find you when they search for your geographical area.

Whether you deal with businesses, professionals, or consumers, everything in your marketing is about them. Each requires different handling and different branding. Each requires their needs to be the focus of your website, your printed materials, and your offers.

It always surprises me when I see other investigators at a lawyer conference who have a booth, signage, and website geared for dealing with consumers. They are clearly in the B2C market, yet they're trying to market in the B2B world or, even more ridiculously, in the P2P world of professional to professional.

Everything from their website and all their leave behinds, brochures and flyers and all the services they render are for private individuals and have **nothing to do with the specific needs of the target audience** they are trying to attract at that conference.

What's worse, in my opinion, is the investigative company that attempts to be a jack of all trades and a master of none. They don't even know if they are B2B, B2C or P2P. They are not a hybrid, because they're trying to do everything for everyone instead of focusing on their specialized knowledge or their geographical exclusivity.

SECTION FIVE: NEEDS ANALYSIS

There is a place for the generalist as I mentioned above. I believe the generalist can be competent when they're the only game in town or are in an out of the way place without much competition. By the sheer fact that they are in an inaccessible area, they can take on all comers. They will be able to take on criminal defense work. They will do skip tracing. They will do cheating wives and husbands, and all the surveillance work for insurance companies because there is no one else in that area to do that work. If that's the case for you, it may make sense to be a hybrid because your competitive advantage is that no one else is there to do the same work as you.

In reality, the only place to go wide with your net of prospects is when you're in the B2C market. You're trying to capture every person in your geographic area with a potential need for a private investigator.

Otherwise, you want to drill very deep into your niche, whether you are B2B or P2P. You want to make sure you are the person they want to come to and that you have the necessary skill sets to be able to meet their needs and to answer their questions.

Tony's Target Audience

Tony has decided to go into the P2P business and is looking to market exclusively to attorneys, certified public accountants, small business owners, and financial planners. Everyone in his target audience can be attracted by his twenty-seven years of expertise in investigations and the ability to understand what the investigative objective is. He has to rely heavily on his NYPD career and contacts. So, his decision to go P2P is also a lifestyle choice of not working nights, weekends or holidays in essentially the Borough of Queens.

Beth's Target Audience

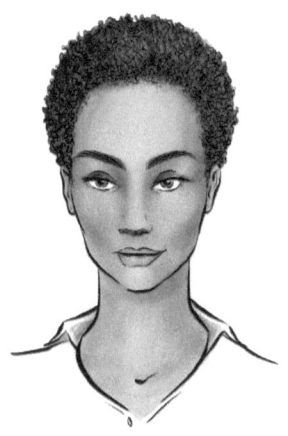

Beth is looking to go to throw a wide net in the B2C ocean. She's looking to provide surveillance services and investigative services as they relate to family law.

She's attempting to attract the private individual before any divorce action is filed or the private individuals looking to modify their custody agreements based upon the miscreant behaviors of their ex-spouse.

She's looking to be a high-volume, low-cost provider to individuals. She will take credit cards and PayPal. She's hoping to scale her business through an excellent website presence and attendance at Chamber of Commerce events. She will institute a referral program from Gyms, Hair, Beauty, Wellness and Nail Salons.

SECTION FIVE: NEEDS ANALYSIS

John's Target Audience

John's B2B business, Independent Special Investigations, LLC was created to meet the needs of the growing community of Special Investigation Units of the property and casualty insurance industry in 1997, as well as the litigation departments of all the casualty claims units of both personal and commercial insurance carriers.

John was very clear that he wanted to work with property and casualty insurance industry and maximize his contacts in his Rolodex to grow his business regionally in the Northeast and Mid-Atlantic states.

Your Target Audience

Who is going to be the end-user as well as the buyer for the services you're going to offer? Are you B2B, P2P or B2C? Keep in mind your 'why' and what gaps that are you filling, as Rocky said. Find some lined paper or create a new document file and fill out as much detail as you can.

A Business with No Customers

This is a story about International Missing Heir Finders, LLC, a business that didn't have customers per se.
"How can that be?" you ask.
Well, John started it as a paying hobby. Eventually, he created a national business named International Missing Heir Finders, LLC. The concept was straightforward. He found probate estates that were recently opened throughout the United States where not all of the rightful heirs had been located. John then went

about determining those rightful heirs and advised them that they were the rightful heirs in an estate of a person who had died and, as an heir, they may be entitled to a portion of the money from that estate. Those heirs then signed a contract before they were advised of who died and where the estate was probated. John also then provided an attorney for them. The heir would pay no expenses. Upon receipt of the funds from the probate court, the attorney would, by contractual agreement, pay International Missing Heir Finders a percentage of the heir's inheritance and the attorney would take their fee from John's share.

You might say the *heirs* were the customers, but they did not come to International Missing Heir Finders asking, "Can you find an estate where I'm entitled to money?" Instead, IMHF came to them, and for a percentage of the inheritance, they would connect the person to that estate and also pay for their legal fees. So in a sense, they were not customers.

John had to sell the heirs on the agreement that they would receive monies from an estate they did not know about. John had to convince Tracers throughout the United States to go out and locate those estates in their local probate courts regularly in exchange for a percentage of the estate when the estate finally settled out. John and his team would do the Forensic Genealogy to locate the heirs. John then had to follow the progress of the estate until the final payout. It was a sweet gig while it lasted, but the business model proved to be too volatile with a high cash burn while waiting for a payout that may or may not happen.

SECTION FIVE: NEEDS ANALYSIS

How to Price Your Services

Regardless of whether you charge clients a fixed budget, flat rate, special offer, discount rate, or by the hour, for purposes of this exercise, you will need to convert them to a per hour rate. If it takes you usually two hours to perform a $500 asset check, your hourly rate is $250 an hour. If you charge $1,000 for eight hours of surveillance, but you have to drive an hour both ways to get there, your ten hours are worth $100 an hour. For all the services you plan to perform, you need to create a weighted-average per hour charge.

In the Northeast, you can go from the low end of $35 an hour for Criminal Defense on court-approved indigent cases to $95-$200 an hour, depending on the specialties and expertise required. What the market will bear in other major metropolitan areas around the country can be very similar to what was just described for the Northeast.

The small towns far away from the metropolitan areas can have pricing from $45-$95 per hour. There's no hard and fast rule as to what is being charged or what the market will bear. What you'll charge per hour for your services should be figured out now before we calculate your critical number. Who is your customer, what is their need, and how much are they willing to pay for your services? How much expertise you bring to the table may allow you to charge premium rates.

When you look at what you will charge for flat rates, hourly, budgets and specials, you have to make an educated guess of how many of each you will sell to arrive at a weighted-average per hour charge.

Projections

$150 Billable Rate (high end)

- 6 hours billed per day generates $900 a day or $4,500 a week.
- Working 48 weeks per year yields $216,000 annual gross
- Less $6,000/month ($72,000/year) in business expenses = $144,000 net
- Multiply by .60 for taxes+SEP = $86,400 annually or $7,200 monthly

$125 Billable Rate (medium)

- 6 hours billed per day generates $750.00 or $3,750 a week.
- Working 48 weeks per year yields $180,000 annual gross
- Less $6,000/month ($72,000/year) in business expenses = $108,000 net
- Multiply by .60 for taxes+SEP = $64,800 annually or $5,400 monthly

$100 Billable Rate (low end)

- 6 hours billed per day generates $600.00 a day or $3,000 a week.
- Working 48 weeks per year yields $144,000
- Less $6,000/month ($72,000/year) in business expenses = $72,000
- Multiply by .65 for taxes+SEP = $48,600 annually or $3,900 monthly

SECTION FIVE: NEEDS ANALYSIS

Critical Number

Take your monthly personal expenses and add to them your monthly business expense, then divide that amount by 4.2 (the number of weeks in an average month). That subtotal is how much your weekly expenses are.

Tony's monthly expense is $7,407 / 4.2 = 1,763.57 weekly. If Tony charges $150 an hour for his services, he needs to bill 11.7 hours weekly. His accountant told him to set aside 1/3 of his revenue for taxes. **So, Tony multiplies his 11.7 hours by 1.33 and comes up with 15.63 hours a week to break even and pay taxes.**

Beth's monthly expenses are $9,459.50 /4.2 = $2,252.26 weekly in the more price-sensitive consumer/commodity pricing. She can only charge a weighted average of $95 per hour for all her services. She must work 23.7 hours to break even, and her accountant told her to set aside 1/4 of her revenue for taxes. **Beth multiplies her 23.7 by 1.25 and sees she needs to work 29.6 hours to break even and pay taxes.** You can see why she needs employees to absorb overhead.

John monthly expenses are $7939.50 / 4.2 = $1,890.46 weekly. John's weighted average for the insurance industry is $131 per hour. John must work 14.4 hours, and his accountant has him setting aside 1/3 of his revenue for taxes. **John multiplies his 14.4 hours by 1.33 for 19.1 hours a week to break even and pay taxes.** John needs employees to absorb overhead as well.

Before you get too giddy that you only have to bill X number of hours a week and you start dreaming about going fishing on three-day weekends, you have to account for administrative hours and non-billable hours that you can't charge the client for. There are marketing hours. There are travel hours that might be charged-off at a reduced rate. There are hours where you involved in managing your business or ownership hours such as doing bookkeeping. The hours spent in your business and working on your business add up quickly. What about the time you take going to conferences or watching webinars to stay sharp and self-improve? What about vacation time and that week you were knocked out with the flu?

> Tip: Add your billable hours up EVERY day and total them at the end of the work week, to know if you made your weekly goal. This is arguably your most critical number.

SECTION SIX: WHAT'S IN A NAME

NAMING YOUR BUSINESS

You're starting your business with a business name; however, you have to think of what that name means when you end your business if you plan to sell that business. You have to think about what that business name means to a potential buyer of your business.

Most importantly, you have to think about what that business name means to the possible customer of your *services*. Does your business name give them the confidence to begin the process of learning to know you, so that they can like and trust you?

Take a moment to visit private investigator companies online. Type in "private detective" or "private investigator" into Google just to give you an idea of what names come up. Would you be comfortable with some of those names on your business card? Is that really the way to present yourself and your business to the outside world? That is the prospect's first impression of your business.

Your website is second. Look at some of the websites. Would you hire that company?

Personally, I think some private detectives do themselves a disservice by playing into the stereotype of the 'Shameless Seamus' or that of the hard-boiled detective. Some detective websites carry the mysterious tough guy thing a little too far.

Take a professional approach to naming your business. Think about the needs of the customer first and your ego second. However, you're entitled to do what you want. Think about it as being synonymous with your name and reputation, though I wouldn't go so far as tattooing that business name or logo on any of your body parts.

There are times when you will name the business after yourself because you are the brand. Whatever you decide, calling your business is something that you need to address at this stage.

As you saw, my first company's name was Independent Special Investigations. It was named for the work that I did. I was an independent, and I did special investigations for the insurance industry. There was an immediate connection with that name. Later on, in another business I owned, I named it Squire Investigations, quite frankly, because I could not come up with a better name. I was transitioning away from the insurance investigations into general local practice and was trying to find the right market niche.

I understand what the naming of a business means now. I later tested a business concept with the name of an online company called Critical Locate Solutions. In our proof of concept, we wanted to provide a premium location service for high-end law firms and corporations. Unfortunately, our research showed the prospects were not dissatisfied enough with their present solutions to change to a higher cost solution, even if it was more effective. The pain of switching providers was more significant than the pain of not finding the party. My proof of concept was not expensive, and it saved me a lot of time, aggravation, and money.

I sell my DVD, *The Ultimate Guide to Taking Statements* from my website *The Department of What Happened*. Clear product name with a catchy website name.

Elm City Detectives was the name of another of my businesses. It clearly explained to the people who lived around the city of New Haven (nicknamed "Elm City") that I was pretty much a local general investigator in the greater New Haven area.

Browser Searches

Your branding and that what you name your company will affect the search algorithms on the various browser networks and a poorly chosen name could place your business on the second page, instead of the coveted first page. Why use a cutesy name that doesn't improve your search rankings?

There are ways to compete to be on the first page of your browser, and those can be very expensive. Rather than bid against companies spending a fortune for the first and second spot, select a good solid name for your business and carefully craft the first several words that are cached in the description of your link.

Domain Names

It's getting harder to find a business name with an available match but try to get a .com name and maybe the .net so that copycats have less of chance of stealing your branding.

Make the name short enough that people will bother to type it. Try to avoid using words such as hallellawfirm where the lack of spaces between the words confuses. Use Whois or GoDaddy.com to see if your domain name is available, and then I recommend going to GoDaddy to register and pay for your domain name.

For domain names, web hosting, and a robust web site builder, 1&1 is also a good choice. HostGator, DreamHost, and Wix.com are similar and have excellent pricing plans as well.

I tend to utilize GoDaddy for my domain names and BlueHost for my web hosting service. I like both GoDaddy and BlueHost

SECTION SIX: WHAT'S IN A NAME

because if I get jammed up on something that is keeping my website from loading or working, I can get a warm body on the phone relatively quickly. They are only two hours' time difference from me, and they speak American English. I'm not trying to be derisive by saying that, but there's something to be said about someone you can understand when they're trying to fix your website.

The next item to consider for your hosting is what is referred to, in the business, as Up Time. You want to make sure that your host's Up Time rate is as close to 100% as possible and that any recovery time is minimal. If they have to do any regular maintenance, make sure they promise it will be at night or on the weekends, when it doesn't cause a problem.

I recommend building your website on a WordPress platform with Thrive Theme Builder. WordPress content management software can be installed on most hosts, including Wix.com, Go Daddy, 1&1, Weebly, SquareSpace, and many others. Wordpress is a platform with a proven track record regarding Up Time that offers seamless integration of patches and fixes along with the ability to take on third-party plug-ins.

Website Builder is a program that allows you to create a website without the need to write or edit code. Website builders are web-based, meaning you don't need to download or install software, you need a browser such as Google Chrome, Mozilla Firefox or Safari, and an Internet connection to start building your website.

Tony's website is the least complicated because of the nature of his business, his branding, and his customer base. In a P2P company, search engine optimization is not as critical. He could pick a domain name from Go Daddy and build it rather quickly with Wix.com or Squarespace. He might need to have some help on WordPress to get started, but mainly those would be my three recommendations for Tony for a rather static site that does not have to have much fresh content.

John's website had to be more interactive. He decided to host a blog and a newsletter for email subscribers to get new information from his offerings. It was important that he had a robust front page which included video testimonials.

John used GoDaddy for the domain name, BlueHost for the host server, WordPress for the platform, and Thrive Architect for the website themes.

It was vital that he could change the content frequently. Refreshing content and good search engine optimization went hand in hand. We can talk about that later, as it is paramount.

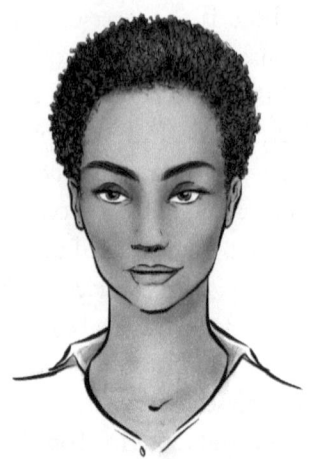

Beth is going B2C. She is competing for eyeballs on the first page of search indexes. She definitely has to be the first or second result on the first page, below the paid ads so people will be attracted immediately to her website where she can entice them into the sales funnel. To do this, she offers her new visitors a free monthly newsletter and ebooks.

She will ask satisfied customers to go on camera and create video testimonials for her. Those videos will feature in a prominent location on her website's home page. In a B2C world, it is probably the most active marketing material you could have.

Her website is the center of her business. Beth utilizes a Go Daddy registered domain, BlueHost for the hosting server, and WordPress with Thrive themes for her website structure. Her website also has to have a robust e-commerce plug-in where customers can enter into agreements, make assignments, and—most importantly—enter credit card or PayPal payments. She needs a very robust platform coming out of the gate.

Beth has little experience with website maintenance, so she hires a reliable IT person available to help her update content, fix bugs, remove dead links, and otherwise keep her website up and running.

The Biggest Mistake Private Investigators Make On Their Websites

Homepage

The biggest mistake that investigators make is that they talk about themselves on their homepage. You might think it's intuitive to tell the customer about yourself so that they will know, like, and trust you.

As much as you think you are selling yourself with your website, you need to be focused on the customer. It's important to understand what the customer's needs are and use your homepage to speak to their needs. That takes practice. Then you follow up with what their wants and desires are.

Your next pages talk about how you can meet their needs. As an example, with Hoda Investigations, one of the first things we listed before our refresh, was a newspaper article about the case involving a wrongful conviction exoneration. That link went to a compelling headline and video. This sends a clear signal to the criminal defense bar that Hoda Investigations works on the most serious criminal cases in the state of Connecticut. That content was immediately followed by four testimonials of well-regarded, highly respected, heavy-hitting lawyers in the state. The message is clear. The best lawyers use the best investigators. You should too. This is the social proof that prospects are looking for. This would be the type of website Tony would want to make as it supplies an immediate know, like, and trust through the first couple of minutes that a visitor spends there.

About Page

The about page is where you talk about your background, your successes, and your history, but again, scripted for the needs of your target market. This is not a place for your resumé. The content needs to reinforce further why the prospect will want to do business with you. Is there anything that is on this page that would turn them off? Please take a look at other websites of private investigators and look at their About pages. Judge them as though you were searching to hire someone with their skill set. We are talking about professionalism in the business here. We're trying to convince people to part with their hard-earned money. We're talking about the lawyers or other businesspersons that are involved in the most important thing on their desk at the time they are shopping for a Professional Private Investigator. Do you want to come across as the Shady Seamus or, worse, a rough and tumble kind of PI?

Whether it is a wife suspecting her husband of cheating on her, an attorney looking to find the facts to support the innocence of his client, or an SIU investigator needing a thorough investigation into a suspicious claim, you have to demonstrate you have repeatedly earned that trust in the past and will give them your best effort. Do you see that promise reflected in the websites of your competitors? It is rare at best.

Most PI websites talk blandly about being everything to everybody. There are other investigators in your geographic area that are a master of the skill that is specific to the needs of your Target Audience. So rather than putting out a watered-down website trying to cast a broader net, be very, very specific about the people you want to work with and speak to them about their needs on your **Services page**.

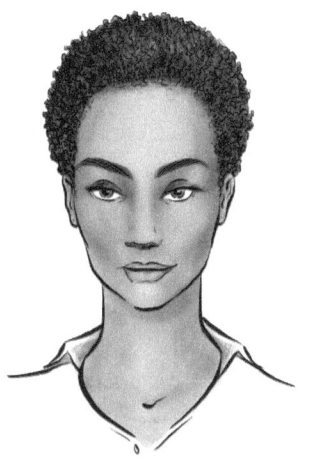

Beth will be very clear that she's working for the little guy. It bears repeating here that she's working for regular people in Family Law cases. Her goal is to provide fast, reliable, and quantifiable results for a fixed price, on a retainer that is price-sensitive for the individuals whom she's trying to attract.

Tony's services have to be very, very specific to all the lawyers, small business owners, and CPAs he wants to work with. He has to show results in the types of cases he wants to work on.

SECTION SIX: WHAT'S IN A NAME

John, in servicing the insurance industry, has to be very clear about special investigations and complex cases. His newsletter and testimonials have to be about achieving great results on those types of cases.

FAQ Page

Hint: If the prospect is on your FAQ page, they are interested.

Here, talk about lowering barriers to making the assignment and overcoming any perceived objections to using your services.

Be sure to provide information on:

- Payment methods accepted
- Reporting: media delivered in person, by email, text, cloud-based file sharing, or phone
- Territory
- Working office hours

Search Engine Optimization (SEO)

Search engine optimization is essential for Beth's B2C segmentation. As described earlier, she has to be first or second on the first page of Google below the paid ads.

As I type this, I am overlooking Lake Winnipesaukee in New Hampshire. I decided to perform a web search for 'New Hampshire private detectives' as if I was a local customer in need of PI services. The first result was a paid ad for an out-of-state company that most likely cannot do investigations in the state of New Hampshire. They did not disclose a person's name or contact. I don't see anything on their website that convinces me they can do work in the Granite State.

Google's keyword tools will help you determine the keywords being used by the websites that have paid ads and decide what words most resonate with what people are searching. You must understand it's not what you want to tell them, it's that you must answer what the prospect believes they are looking for. Those keywords typed in by your target audience have to be a natural part of the content of your website, not in a repetitive fashion, but in a way that makes it clear that you are concentrating on the prospect's needs and not on what you do best.

In checking for "New Hampshire investigators," a private investigative firm from out of the country comes up as the first paid ad. Really? Certainly they are not in a position to be able to assist the people in either Manchester or Concord, New Hampshire's larger cities, or anywhere else for that matter.

Sales Funnels

As the Internet matures, it is becoming clear to all marketers that, by creating a sales funnel from the time you generate an inbound lead, to qualifying the prospect, and then bringing them through the sales process, can all be done digitally within a properly structured website. This is done very expertly by all those businesses selling goods on the Internet. How many times have you gone through an online sale and ended up adding something to your cart that was steeply discounted?

The same technique applies to the businesses of both Beth and John. Their websites will allow for an up-sell opportunity for an additional investigation that is presented as a logical add-on to the investigation initially requested. This up-sell is a moneymaker and a valuable service provided to the customer that they did not initially think (or even consider they needed).

Autoresponders

Persons coming to your website which will give you their email in exchange for valuable content can be put into an email auto response sequence to walk them through getting additional content or more value in their engagement.

This helps the prospect move from learning about you to knowing, liking, and trusting you.

Digital reports, newsletters, and video webinars all move the lead to become a prospect and hopefully to a buyer.

Email Capture

Mailerlite, MailChimp, Convert Kit, and Infusionsoft are all services that allow you to capture emails and create email campaigns. Just starting out, I would recommend Mailerlite or MailChimp. Their free versions are easy to set up and hard to break.

The guides that AppSumo publishes on capturing emails, and how to craft your own emails, headlines, and content is worth spending time with.

The phrase **know, like, and trust** is very much embedded in the sales process before a person will decide that they want to do business with you.

In all cases, people are people. Whether they are a personal consumer, claims manager, business person, or an attorney, they need to have a sense of knowing whom they're dealing with and liking and trusting you before they'll take the next step.

SECTION SEVEN: MARKETING FOR THE INVESTIGATOR

DEVELOP A PLAN

There are many different names for the act of securing your customers leading them through the entire sales process. Sometimes the method is called the sales cycle or the sales funnel, but make no mistake about it; the marketing plan you develop must be based upon behaviors you can the scale and replicate. This is how your business will grow.

The process falls into a very simple straightforward beginning, middle, and end. It starts with the lead generation to either attract prospects with your message (called inbound marketing), or you reach out to them with some way of helping to meet their needs (outbound marketing). There are whole volumes written on both methods, but for some business models, one way may be more effective than the other.

Inbound marketing works for companies providing surveillance on cheating spouses, whereas with law firms, more success is met with outbound marketing that reaches out to prospective clients and makes them aware of your services and how you can meet their needs.

Once you **generate leads**, either through inbound or outbound marketing, or some combination of both, you will **qualify the prospect** to determine if you can meet their needs with the services you provide, at a price that would be acceptable to them.

During this phase, you want to provide **assurances** to the prospect that you can solve their problem, either by providing services for them or by connecting them with services provided by your affiliates or associates. We get into affiliate and associate discussions later on in the series, but they allow you to assure prospective clients that you can help get them closer to a solution for their specific problem.

Ask them **clarifying questions** about what their problem is after you offer them the above assurances. Too many salespeople across all types of businesses will launch into a sales pitch before understanding completely what their prospects needs are. This is a mistake. Every minute the prospect spends explaining the situation to you is one more minute they have invested in you being the solution to their problems.

Depending on the complexity of the situation, and after you have clarified their needs, tailor a **presentation** to them (which is probably the least amount of time spent in the conversation as opposed to the most).

Alternatively, you can offer them a ready-made solution, such as a flat rate. You know from work you've done in the past how to put together a budget for a flat rate. Based on the required skill sets and the time you know each will take to complete, and the related expenses, you can estimate that flat rate with some certainty. Plan for at least a 50% profit margin on that time and expense in order to make it viable.

You may receive **objections**. This is where you spend time going over the prospect's needs, explaining how your solutions meet those needs. They begin to understand the benefit they will receive from having the work done professionally and at a cost that can be agreed upon.

Tip: Sometimes the approach to overcoming objections is to understand the exact reason for not making a decision and help the prospect overcome that resistance. Too many times you may hear the objection is about money, but in reality, it could be having to live with the consequences of their decision. They are afraid of moving forward. Sometimes, you have to paint a picture of what the future looks like once they possess the information.

It would help if you made the decision simple for them and then you seamlessly flow into **getting the assignment**. You start the process of taking the information from the individuals, no differently than a car salesman would begin the application process for a car loan.

You now agree on pricing. It is here where it can be as simple as a handshake, getting a retainer signed, or filling out the contract.

However, wait, there's more. Once you've reached an agreement on the original assignment and the customer is relaxed and ready to move forward with the task, talk about other skills sets that you possess for the logical leads that would be tremendously beneficial to the customer to further their goals.

This is the **up-sell** I have mentioned a couple of times, and in the business of private investigations, it means taking an assignment and increasing the number of investigative steps, while providing more value to the customer.

Sometimes the up-sell includes a discount for an additional service or flat rate. Sometimes it involves expanding the initial scope of the investigation to be more comprehensive. This is an opportunity to increase the lifetime value of that new client after you agree on the initial assignment.

During your work for the client, there are times when the upsell will occur after the initial work is done to your client's satisfaction and because the investigation uncovers additional information or leads. Following up on those can increase the value of the case by providing the customer with additional services. Sometimes the upsell is done during the initial sales process. Sometimes the upsell comes after the work is done and has exceeded your client's expectations. While they're delighted with the work, further opportunities to expand the investigation are more accessible to digest, and they are open to engaging you for additional work. You might think this is not part of the sales cycle, but it is.

After you receive the assignment and agree on the price, talk with the client about their **preferred communication method. This is probably more important than the work itself.** Establishing communication expectations from the onset will increase the client's satisfaction with your services.

Ask whether they prefer email, text, or phone calls for status updates, and how often they want to receive updates. A question like that goes a long way towards improving the customer's satisfaction quotient.

Many Private Investigators think that receiving payment for completed work is the end of the sales cycle, but it isn't. Two additional aspects of the sales cycle are essential to the private investigator, especially one starting their business.

The first is asking for **testimonials.** Second is asking for **referrals.**

When the client is so happy with the work you've done as if they're willing to leave a testimonial, a well-formed testimonial spells out the specific benefit they received for a real need they had and how you were able to solve their problem uniquely. **When asking for a testimonial, give the client an example and let them adapt it to their case.**

Customers will often only be willing to include their first name and last initial in their testimonial. Other clients are less bashful and will grant you use of their full name and title, depending on the type of work you're performing and the type of client they are.

Getting a testimonial for a job well done is a crucial aspect of your marketing.

Hint: Upon receipt of payment, make a phone call to the client thanking them for the payment. Ask them how happy they were with the work you did and then, assuming they had no complaints, ask them for a testimonial or send them a customer satisfaction survey with an ask, "Can I quote you?"

Testimonials should not be left up to the client to decide how to word. You should send them a brief sample. Let them know you plan to use the testimonial on your website or in your marketing materials.

Too many investigators are bashful and do not ask for testimonials. They're happy they've been paid and are too busy working cases to ask. However, you must make testimonials part of your marketing strategy.

The more **social proof** you have that you meet the needs of your target audience, the easier it is for prospects to know, like, and trust you.

After you receive payment on a couple of cases from a happy client, there is nothing wrong with calling that client and asking for **referrals**.

This is, again, something investigators are loath to do and I don't understand it. Quite frankly, you've done an excellent job for this client, and your work shines. Their needs were met at a fair price. They're thrilled with the results, very happy with the effort that you expended in their investigation and, although they might have some difficult things to deal with; as a result, you got them the straight facts. In their minds, you are the person anyone should go to for that same issue.

Merely ask who else might they think of who would benefit from your services.

Just ask for permission to contact the other person, or have them introduce you to the other person.

By having them making contact with their friend or colleague, you get the benefit of both a testimonial and a referral. Better still, tell them their friend or colleague should mention their name to you for a **10% referral discount.** That is a double win for your client and their referral.

This has the benefit of that client becoming a true fan of your business. If all this sounds daunting, take it one step at a time. After all, how do you eat an elephant? One bite at a time.

In the next book in this series, we cover entirely marketing for private investigators, with techniques that will take less than five hours a week.

For now, plan to devote 10% of the time you will spend on your business marketing your business. If you prepare for a fifty-hour week, five hours of weekly marketing effort should be a rule of thumb.

Sadly, most investigators spend zero hours marketing after their website is built. Then they complain that they don't have any customers, that they're scraping for customers, that they have to accept any customer that walks in the door, or that they have to offer ridiculously discounted rates to keep the lights on.

This is a huge part of why 85% of private investigators fail to renew their license after their second year of being in business.

Here's the other axiom that is probably the most beneficial advice I've ever received.

The diet that you do is better than the diet you should do, but don't.

The exercise that you do is better than the exercise you should do, but don't.

The marketing that you do is better than the marketing you should do, but don't.

This is a time to think about the marketing method you feel most comfortable with, one that aligns your business with your target audience and puts your skill sets in direct line with their needs.

This is how you begin promoting your business. When I ask other investigators how much marketing they do, they say they do some marketing and explain what it is. I ask them to tell me how many hours a week they spend on that and they offer a guesstimate. In reality, they really don't know. I'm going to tell you now to track your marketing hours as you do your billable hours so that, week after week, you know whether or not you're following the most important numbers for your business.

I place billable hours first and my marketing hours second. If billable hours drop, it has an immediate effect on cash flow. If you cut the number of marketing hours, the income drop is not quick, but it does impact your ability to attract and retain customers to put more cases in your pipeline later on.

Tracking your marketing activity is extremely important, and though it is only mentioned here briefly, I go into more detail later in book two of this series, *How to Market Your Private Investigations Business*.

It would help if you utilized a customer relationship management software. There are several different products on the market, ranging from free, to relatively inexpensive, to very expensive. It can be as simple as a Google Sheets spreadsheet or another type of free customer relationship software with minimal features and benefits. If your needs are more complex, or specific, there are other paid CRM solutions such as ACT! for use with Windows operating systems. InSightly is a very robust CRM that I use to keep track of my leads, which works well in the Apple environment.

A higher end CRM called Hubspot has integrations with email and other platforms, reducing repetitive key stroking across platforms and how many screens you have to toggle between.

For more business-to-business severe ventures there is Salesforce.

The spectrum of your CRM options ranges from free to expensive. The option that will work best for you to track and grow your business will depend on what your needs are.

Full disclaimer: I still keep a simple spreadsheet of newly acquired customers and their email addresses. Each time I get a new customer, I put their name into one column, their email address in the second column and then use either **MailerLite** or **MailChimp** to send out any mailings I have. I send out newsletters, special announcements, or occasional specials that I run. I keep all my prospects in my **Insightly** database.

Several years ago, when I was forced to rethink my business model, I decided I would run my business almost exclusively from an iPad, and I left the Windows environment. I now run 90% of my business from my iPad. The other 10% is bookkeeping with my same accountant, who prefers I do my accounting on QuickBooks in Windows. I kept an old Dell PC for that reason, but otherwise, I run my entire business from an iPad.

Utilizing an app called iThoughts HD. I used the app's Genogram template to identify what my marketing streams were going to be and to see how effective those marketing streams were, in terms of both the number of prospects as well as conversions from leads, to prospects, to actual clients.

From my earliest clients, I received referrals to other prospects, who later became clients. The Genogram template kept a genealogy chart of an entire 'family' of clientele that entered my database as referrals by great, great, great, great, grandparent clients.

I decided that each marketing stream would be like the great, great, great, great granddaddy. I was able to track each marketing stream of leads, prospects, and customers. I continued to do that for several years. I was able to show what was working and what wasn't visually. The Genogram allowed me to go in daily to see what leads I needed to contact that day, and what I had said to those leads previously. It allowed me to grow my business and see where my company was coming from, all from a $12 app. You could simulate the organization in a spreadsheet by assigning an alpha designation for your marketing stream, like C for Chamber of Commerce or P for Public Defenders office. Then you could easily sort and filter your leads, prospects, and customers.

This CRM allowed me to track the numbers and my five hours a week of marketing my business. I did this marketing between 8:30 am and 9:30 am, Monday through Thursday, and then a recap of activity Friday and Saturday for the remaining hour. At 9:30 in the morning, I finished my marketing chores for the day and was able to go on to do the rest of my administrative and billable hours.

If I waited until too late in the afternoon to do my marketing, I might be too tired or, if I had an excellent billing day, I might think I really didn't need to do any marketing because my cases were going so well. By getting my marketing out of the way in the morning, which was the best time for me, I was able to then return phone calls during the course of the day and my marketing would fit seamlessly with my travel time.

Marketing Plan

At this point, I would keep your marketing plan on one page. In keeping with the advice I quoted above, making a one-page plan is better than the multi-page marketing plan that you should make, but don't.

An additional benefit is that a one-page marketing plan can be kept somewhere in front of or near you; somewhere where it can stare you in the face every day. This plan will serve as a constant reminder of your **Why, How, and What.** Keep them front and center in your workspace so you can focus on what you're trying to accomplish on a daily and weekly basis. This works better than a plan that looks beautiful after you spent hours crafting, only to bury it in your desk drawer where it is forgotten. An out of sight marketing plan doesn't do anything for you.

Use the **S.M.A.R.T.** technique to spell out what your marketing will look like. S.M.A.R.T. is an acronym for Specific, Measurable, Achievable, Results, and Time. Each heading gives you direction how to craft your marketing actions. Pick goals which are specific, measurable, actionable/achievable, results-oriented, and have a time frame for completion. If you make your one-page marketing plan S.M.A.R.T. compliant, you will be much closer to achieving your goals. Remember, the marketing you do is better than the marketing you should do, and don't.

Ten percent of your work time, spent marketing, could be the difference between success and failure. Take the time to understand what your marketing approach to your target market is, and continuously and methodically tweak it until you see the results you're looking for.

Not all new business people are marketing geniuses coming out of the starting gate, but getting your Private Investigation business to lift off the ground is a matter of marketing, and a case of seeing what works, disregarding the things that don't, or tweaking things to make them better.

Unfortunately, too many marketing gurus and business coaches want to convince you an investment in their marketing course can fix your problems. In reality, the fixing has to be based upon their advice, but you have to do the work to get the desired result.

Most times, marketing plans fail because you are not aligning your skill sets with your customer's needs and, then, you are not completing the sales cycle to convert leads to prospects to clients to referrals. Most marketing campaigns fail because they are poorly conceived and executed.

"Where do I find my customers?" is always asked, but rarely are the answers easy to tease out.

The time spent making your marketing plan is best spent on making one that is Achievable. This is probably the most important of the of the five letters in the S.M.A.R.T. acronym.

Failure to make a sustained marketing effort is probably one of the most significant causes for a private investigation business to fold.

After the initial push where a PI meets with some success, they get swallowed up in the administrative and billable activity associated with providing top-notch service. The investigator fails to keep up their marketing, thinking they do not need to go further with marketing and forget to ask for testimonials or referrals. In short order, the pipeline dries up, and the investigators are left scratching their heads, wondering how to get more customers. By that time, it may be too late. Cash flow has dropped to dangerous levels, and they have to abort the mission.

SECTION SEVEN: MARKETING FOR THE INVESTIGATOR

Sample Marketing Plan 20XX

- Daily calls for 60 minutes replaced by actual appointments.
- Email inspirational story to clients with a newsletter every quarter.
- Track in CRM and Genogram. Continue to use Martindale-Hubbell lists.
- Thank every client for their business and ask for more. Mention Flat rates.
- Go back and sell Flat Rate Statements and Locates as Introductory offer to all phoned prospects that did not buy last year.
- Create Asset check Email Blast in Mail Chimp for clients, then for prospects.
- Test Collateral in 20XX seminars. Track conversions.
- Make one daily referral request of my clients.
- After each 20XX success story, craft a testimonial letter for the client.
- Get the assignment. What do you need? What have you already done? When do you need it by? What's your Budget? Set a budget then talk up-sell.
- End of the year Holiday Greeting cards get lost in all the traffic. Get a jump on your competitors and send your hand-signed greetings at Thanksgiving.

The above is just a sample marketing plan, mostly geared to the P2P business Tony is involved in, to give you an idea of how to be **specific**, how to **measure** your successes, **achieve** your goals, the **results** you're looking for, and the **time** frame involved, following the S.M.A.R.T. process. It could be easily adapted for the B2B model John was contemplating in his 1997 launch as well.

Beth's marketing plan for the B2C category needs to be focused on inbound marketing. The clientele she wants is out browsing the Internet for investigative solutions for their personal needs. Additionally, she has to be very adept in the cultivation of testimonials and a referral network based upon happy customers. Much of her marketing time will be spent tweaking the search engine optimization, making sure she stays on the first page and that the keywords she utilizes match the keywords being used by prospects to search for the services she renders.

She has to continue to work on her website pages, walking the lead through the sales funnel to the place where they are willing to leave their information in a **Contact** form, click the **Chat Now** button, or make a phone call to discuss their case with Beth. She has to keep fresh content on her site with suitable free reports, e-books, and newsletters. Part of her testimonials should be a video of satisfied customers. This is crucial in a B2C market. She needs to show real people give compelling testimonials as to why the prospect should take the next step.

Part of Beth's marketing plan in the greater Austin area is to ingratiate herself with persons in the **Chamber of Commerce Leads Groups** or in the **BNI Business Network International** groups.

Beth needs to grow a list of affiliate marketers, people who would receive a commission for referring prospects that result in paying customers. Beth wants to concentrate on leads from upscale hair salons, gyms, wellness spas, and nail and beauty shops.

SECTION SEVEN: MARKETING FOR THE INVESTIGATOR

> *If you want to hunt wildebeest, you go where the wildebeest drink.*
>
> One PI I know joined co-ed softball leagues in up-scale towns and sponsored teams with his company's name on the team shirts. Right demographic for fidelity investigations, for sure. This would be an excellent tip for Beth. Are the professionals in your state-mandated to get continuing education credits at seminars? Sponsor a seminar or have a table. Do the businesses you want to do business with go to a trade association meeting? Do they have local chapters? Sponsor the happy hour. Guess what, you get happy prospects.

AIDA

This acronym spells out the sales process of moving a prospect through the process of becoming a customer.

Attention: Get the attention and keep the attention of the prospect

Interest: Create interest with how you can meet the prospect's needs

Desire: Make compelling arguments for the prospect to want your service to the exclusion of others.

Action: The Call to Action is most often ignored in most marketing content generated by Private Investigators. Stop the pain! Don't Delay! Act Now! Ask About Our (Season) Special.

Your marketing content language should fall into one of these four categories. Any discussion of marketing that fails to include the acronym AIDA would be lacking. It is the overlay on any of your marketing activities.

DEVELOP A PLAN

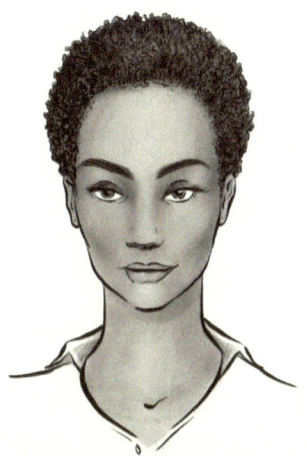

In Beth's case, her website captures attention immediately with a strong headline or sub-headline that details the benefits she provides, as well as stating the problem she can solve. To create interest in her services, she includes an informational video and testimonials. Before she was able to gather testimonial videos, she displayed thumbnail portraits of the persons next to written testimonials.

To create a desire for her services, Beth shows how much it may cost for another investigative firm to provide the same services and then shows how her prices are much more user-friendly and reliable. Beth argues the difference between an open-ended hourly rate which could drain the prospect's checkbook, versus a Flat Rate or Budget contract. Again, she includes more testimonials debunking objections while reinforcing the benefits of choosing her services.

Most importantly for Beth, is an attractive call to action. She includes a contact form with room for the prospect to spell out the assignment. It even consists of a boilerplate contract and an e-commerce button to secure a refundable deposit for a free consultation by credit card, PayPal, or bank draft.

Can you imagine the client going through the sales process, filling out the assignment information, then signing the terms of an agreement (boilerplate retainer), then providing a credit card for the fixed amount on the initial assignment? Beth wakes up the following morning, and she has in her inbox a completed task and a retainer, requiring only a confirmation by email, text, or phone, as the client has specified.

All of that to me seems to be a pretty good way of making money.

SECTION SEVEN: MARKETING FOR THE INVESTIGATOR

Tony wonders all about this marketing and selling stuff. He thought he could do it, but now he is having second thoughts. After a short stint working in the trades as a laborer after high school, he decided to join the police department. What he feels about selling was gleaned from roles played Al Pacino in Glengarry Glen Ross and Leonardo DiCaprio in the Wolf of Wall Street—not exactly right role models.

Selling has a bad connotation to him. Then there is the barrage of telemarketing calls on his phone and pop-ups when he does a google search for the Mets score.

Worse, as he starts asking professionals how they market, he gets a blizzard of answers and, as a trained investigator, realizes they are as clueless as he is.

How do they stay in business? he wonders.

Tony realizes this is a weakness and his own pre-conceptions are getting in the way. He knows he will make mistakes until he feels comfortable with listening to his clients' needs and learning how to meet them.

DEVELOP A PLAN

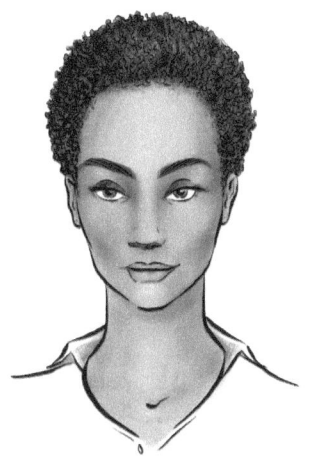

Beth is coming into this sales pipeline process with open eyes. She says very clearly, "My branding, marketing, and sales materials are all about the consumer. My services will allay their fears and help them with the decisions that they need to make."

She is building her business around her Why, How, and What. She looks to other Service related e-Commerce sites and hones her process to capture eyeballs and convert leads to prospects. This is the new language she has to learn. Sitting in on prisoner of war debriefing sessions in Afghanistan taught her how to learn new languages, and now, as then, she has to learn the new language of selling.

SECTION EIGHT: THE BUSINESS OF YOUR BUSINESS

WHAT IS YOUR BUSINESS ENTITY GOING TO BE?

Sole Proprietorship

You may want to consider the unincorporated option, sole proprietorship, if you don't have any employees and the business is just you. This is an ideal choice. Profit from your company goes to your personal tax returns, and all of your business expenses are deductible. The revenue and expenses are written upon an IRS form called a schedule C.

Since you will be filing a Schedule C at the end of the year, you'll need to keep track of every receipt and go through your expenses carefully with your accountant and bookkeeper.

My preferred paper method is to remove all the expenses and credit card statements from my monthly folders and then aggregate them by the type of expense. With an accounting program, you need to transfer the information from your program to the Schedule C. Many bookkeeping programs, like QuickBooks, have integration with tax prep apps like Turbo Tax.

SECTION EIGHT: THE BUSINESS OF YOUR BUSINESS

Quarterly Estimates

You need to track all your income so that you can pay your estimated taxes quarterly. Some people suggest that 33% be set aside of each check your company receives. I'm in a high tax state of Connecticut, and 33% works well for me.

Partnerships

This is a straightforward discussion for me, because of the way that Tony, Beth, or John have set up their businesses. None involve a partnership.

A partnership is a business formation you can aspire to after you've already launched and established a running private investigations business. Consider adding a partner or two when doing so will give your business a synergetic boost when the sum is greater than the parts. Most partnerships, however, are a dilution of assets and capital and run the risk of imploding because no agreement was hammered out in the beginning. Most marriages end in divorce and most partnerships, where even more effort is made to spell out responsibilities and expectations, also tend to fall that way.

It is difficult to imagine how your business can grow in its earliest stages when it is dependent on a partner whom you have no control over.

Limited Liability Companies

An LLC, or limited liability company, is a popular option with small business owners because it has even more significant advantages than an S Corp., especially if you want to offer employees a part of the business. This is now the most popular legal entity type as it is the best of both a C or an S corporation without the restrictions. A single member limited liability company is not allowed in some states, however, so you should check with your accountant to determine whether or not you can form a single member LLC.

Forming an LLC puts you at arm's length, away from any liability action that can be taken against you or, as you grow your business, taken against your company because of the actions of your employees.

S or C Corporations

A corporation confers limited liability to the corporation and not the members. The individual assets are protected in the absence of exceptional circumstances like a fraud. C Corporations are relatively easy and inexpensive to form but may be subject to **double taxation**. This means that the corporation pays tax on the profit and then the shareholders pay tax on the money they take home from the profit. You can avoid the double taxation issue with an S corporation. With an S corp, you maintain the protection from personal liability, and you avoid the double taxation issue that often arises with a C Corporation. The S Corporation operates like any corporation with the establishments of officers, directors, and shareholders. You do need to file a great deal of paperwork like a C corporation. It is more expensive than the unincorporated options because you need to hire a lawyer and an accountant to file the paperwork for you, but for small businesses, it is an option. Listing "Inc., P.C." after your company name in the B2B world confers some additional legitimacy as the prospect can verify your corporate status.

Some restrictions apply, and you should review the details with the professional who files your taxes for you. I'm not a lawyer nor an accountant, nor do I play either on TV.

My feeling is that an LLC or limited liability company is the preferred route should you plan on growing your business to include employees or subcontractors that could all bring liability to your company with their actions. However, if you plan to be a solo operator, then a Sole Proprietorship gives you the ease of the only business formation you'll need, but understand the risk.

This writer chose to create an LLC which allows for business growth with employees.

Employee Identification Number (EIN)

This is a requirement by most of the states to tax your revenue and is required by the IRS. Your bank would also need an EIN if you're planning to open a checking account in the business's name.

The Internal Revenue Service does require an EIN number for your sole proprietorship when classified as a limited liability company, Partnership, C Corporation, or S Corporation.

It makes sense for you to secure this number after you have named your business so that you're able to do your banking and secure credit cards under that name.

Banking

It is strongly urged that you create a separate checking account for your business operating account and separate all your business deposits and expenses from your personal income and expenses.

For the same reason, it makes sense to have a separate business credit card.

Your choice of credit cards depends on whether or not you want cash back or airplane miles. Depending on what your lifestyle goals are, there are some excellent airline mileage cards with no travel restrictions such as Capital One, and some great cashback cards such as a Discover or Amazon Prime card which gives you cashback and discounts while making purchases from preferred stores. (I do not have any affiliation with any of these financial institutions; I am just offering these as suggestions.)

Additionally, it makes sense to have a second business account that you keep solely for retainers that you receive and for money set aside for your quarterly federal and state tax estimates. The more you keep these monies segregated from your operating accounts, the less you will be tempted to use this money to meet cash flow.

Part of the reason to keep retainers out of your operating account is if you have to return the retainer, as per the terms of your agreement. That you have the money on hand when the retainer is fully earned out, you're able to transfer that money into your operating account then. Law firms are required by the state laws to have trust accounts for their clients, and they work off their retainers by moving the funds from their trust account into their operating account. This is a good practice to get into from the beginning to keep yourself out of problematic situations.

Debit Card

Your bank will offer you a credit card that has a debit card capability, and it makes sense to have it so you can withdraw funds out of an ATM for Cash or miscellaneous expenses, without incurring fees for cash advances against your credit card. My recommendation is to choose a bank that has many branch offices in your area of operation as well as at least one that is close to your residence.

Even though more and more banking is done electronically as mobile apps replace the need for a personal visit to a bank branch, it is good to have a relationship with your local bank manager and that relationship could do wonders for you later on. Case in point: I was traveling out of the country and received a call from my bank manager and told the bank had made a mistake and deposited funds into the wrong checking account. I received a contact from the payroll company saying the payroll checks would bounce. There was nothing I could do from Florence, Italy at the time this happened! However, because of my good relationship with the bank manager, the bank made sure the funds were put into the proper account and paid my expense to have the payroll company issue the checks on a special run.

By establishing a relationship with your bank manager, you're in a position to take advantage of offerings at the bank, such as a credit line and home equity loan should there be an opportunity for you to grow your business. That is not to say I'm recommending you take out a credit line or home-equity line for your business. Rule of thumb would be not to engage in a home equity loan or a line of credit if your business is in trouble. This is not the way to address the issues while your company is hemorrhaging money. First, look at a viable plan to downsize before you take on additional debt. What happens, unfortunately, in most cases, is that a home equity loan or a line of credit is extended and that extra money doesn't fix the problem, and now you have additional debt.

Hiring An Accountant

Your relationship with your bank manager is only second to your relationship with your accountant. When interviewing an accountant, make sure that they are a certified public accountant (CPA). Confirm that they offer services related to small businesses and have them give you the names of other sole proprietorship's or small companies they deal with. Request permission to contact them and see if they are satisfied with the services of their accountant.

Be sure you know how often your accountant wants to meet with you, and whether or not you're using an accountant in combination with a bookkeeper. There are times when an accountant will offer a bookkeeper at a reduced rate as part of your relationship. You'll also want to know how many times you need to meet with the bookkeeper and/or accountant to do the bookkeeping.

You want to know exactly who is going to be working on your books and if the accountant you meet is going to be the exact person that will be filing your tax returns.

Also of importance is what bookkeeping system they plan to use. My accountant is an expert in QuickBooks and, although QuickBooks is one of the more expensive options for me, I am happier that my accountant is satisfied with his preferred software as he can save time fixing problems I create with my record-keeping or bookkeeping.

Most importantly, you need to know that they can go toe-to-toe with the IRS when faced with paying interest and penalties. Also, you want to make sure your accountant can explain to the IRS any honest mistakes that were made and be able to amend the tax return at the lowest possible additional cost to yourself. We are not talking about evading taxes here, but avoiding paying more taxes than required by law.

Is your accountant available for phone calls or emails? There have been times when I've been able to get a text reply from my accountant on a Saturday within a few minutes of making the request. This is the kind of relationship you will like to establish, as well.

I would say that after about 18 or 19 years with the same accountant, his services are pricey. However, I will also say the services he provides me are priceless, in that I know where I stand at the half-year mark, I know where I stand just before the holidays when he gives me an idea of where I'm going to be on tax day. I know he also helps me understand my tax liabilities for the upcoming year. There are no surprises on tax day.

I think of both my bank manager and my accountant as professionals that I can use as sounding boards with my business, even after 22 years of being in business.

SECTION EIGHT: THE BUSINESS OF YOUR BUSINESS

Licensing, Bonding, And Insurance

When you apply for your license, it is a good idea to have the name of your company in mind, as they will ask for it. It also makes sense to know the type of business you're going to be, as different states have different dues for licensing based upon the type of business organization your private investigation business will be.

It also makes sense to have the type of business in your business name, such as Arrow Investigations, Inc. Willis & Associates, LLC for your EIN and on your business bank account.

Have the name ready when you go for professional liability insurance as required by your state licensing board (you should also think about it, even if it's not needed).

Think about the insurance as being precisely what it is: an insurance policy for your professional conduct. You're about to enter into a business that, if you're a sole proprietor, may expose your equity in your home and your other assets to a frivolous civil suit.

I carry a $1 million in an Errors and Omissions policy, with a $2 million aggregate, so that, should multiple people make claims against my business for a particular incident, there will be enough coverage there to handle that event.

Many states require bonding. I would suggest you make contact with your local private investigator association or the state Private Investigator association and talk with the leaders of that association. Please introduce yourself and ask questions about whom they prefer for their errors and omissions coverage, professional liability coverage, and their bonding. Some state associations have secured discounts with preferred vendors, and you might try joining your state organization. The discount from the insurance coverage may make up for the cost of your membership with that organization.

Reporting

I do 99% of my reports on my iPad and have a template that creates an invoice once a report is finished. Both the invoice and report are sent either by mail or by email to the client. The invoice is then manually entered into QuickBooks under the customer account. However, other investigators invoice directly through their QuickBooks or other accounting software. Many of these software allow for electronic payment, yet the float time on having access to the funds can be longer.

For longer reports, you may consider a transcriptionist or use a software titled Dragon Dictate. I dictated this book into a portable recorder and transcribed it through Dragon Dictate. It saves time and effort versus typing voluminous reports by hand.

The other thing about dictation is that, if you're working on multiple cases during the day and are running and gunning, as they say, you may not have time to sit after each event and chronicle it, but it might be easier to pick up a $40 digital recorder and record that case into a digital folder named for that case. Then, at the end of all your dictation on that case, put it through a transcription software like Dragon.

Dragon Dictate is designed for the Windows platform. This writer uses an older version for Apple and finds he is still delighted with the accuracy of the transcription.

What follows is more an investigative tip than a procedural tip with reporting, but the reality is the longer you wait to compile your reports after the actual work is done, the more a report may look like a synopsis, and many of the essential facts you gathered may be lost in the truncated reporting weeks later. Additionally, the information you possess that day may get lost if it's not recorded correctly.

In the early years of my investigative career, I had a separate dictation tape for every single file I worked on. The transcriptionist would receive a tape after the case and transcribe it from beginning to end. I was able to reuse the analog tapes.

From a billing standpoint, being able to dictate your reports while you were traveling on your cases reduces the administrative time spent on your cases. At the end of the day, if you use some of your travel time to dictate your reports, you will allow for more billable time and more marketing time, rather than being tethered behind your laptop, typing out what you did that night or the previous day.

Customer Relationship Management Software (CRM)

Long gone are the days of a Rolodex, where you kept your stack of business cards. That ship has sailed. If you wish to minimize your time administrating to marketing chores then using a customer relationship management software is imperative.

By keeping track of your leads, your prospects, and your customers, you're able to know when to follow up with them, to move them further down the sales funnel, or to ask them for testimonials or referrals. You can use CRM's email compilation features to provide your prospects and customers with newsletters, announcements, or seasonal sales.

At the time of writing, I am offering a special 10% discount for new customers on our flat rates between now and Labor Day. It is our summer special.

An email blast went out to 279 prospects. It took 45 minutes to create the sales copy in a **MailChimp** campaign, and it has already netted several thousand dollars and a half dozen new clients. If I did not retain the name of the prospects and their email addresses, I would not have had that opportunity for any of that return. By keeping this data in a simple spreadsheet where I can filter between leads, prospects, and customers, it's not difficult to filter or sort in a way that allows me to easily cut-and-paste email addresses into the proper marketing campaign.

I use a combination of Excel spreadsheets for customers and **Insightly** CRM for leads and prospects. It's not difficult to set up a spreadsheet or to all learn the basics of a CRM software package such as Insightly or **ACT**.

The time you spend key-stroking the prospects' information into your CRM is recouped by the long-term value of all the prospects you received by following them up with regular marketing.

I have followed up with some prospects as long as three years after first meeting them and have received a significant income because the time was right for them, even though it was not right for them at the time of the initial engagement. Over the years, they became disenchanted with their previous provider, or their previous provider moved away from Connecticut, got sick, died, or retired, and by having regular and ongoing contact with me, they accepted the latest invitation to engage.

Assignment log- keeping track of your assignments and their report due dates is imperative to make sure you don't lose your assignments and that you're on top of your work. You are providing regular and ongoing status reports to your clients until the cases are completed. **This is the number one reason why professionals will give up on their present provider. They are dissatisfied with the lack of regular reporting and communication.**

Another purpose for keeping an assignment log is to see where your work is coming from geographically, by type of work, and by customers. How many cases your different customers are giving you is a significant detail in the B2B world as well as in the P2P world, though not so much in the B2C business to consumer sphere, as many times this is a one-off engagement. However, keeping a record of when you receive these cases, how often you receive them, the type of assignments that you receive, the money that you make on the cases, and successful up-sells are all important metrics to follow to make sure you know how your business is performing.

If you're doing 15% better than you had budgeted for the year or, conversely if you are doing 15% less than you planned for the year, what is the reason for this? Can you point to the reason not only from your accounting software but also from your assignment log? With both your assignment log and your customer invoicing, you can gauge the effectiveness of your marketing.

At the time of this writing, I compared the first two quarters of this year to our budget projections, and then to the same quarter of the previous year. I was able to immediately pinpoint our growth and where I have been falling behind.

The loss of income during that period was not made up by the marketing efforts in my other marketing streams, so it was decided a new marketing stream would be would be added to my business model to see if I could the pump up the numbers for the second half of the year. However, without having an assignment log, you are left scratching your head wondering why things are happening as they are.

Your assignment log not only points out what is not going right—which is very, very important—but it also helps to understand what's going well and what you could do to make what's going well even better. Here's a chance for you to leverage your business from satisfactory to above average by applying more effort and more monies towards the things that are working.

If you don't know what's working and why then you don't know how to allocate resources accordingly.

Simple column headings such as date opened, date closed, which investigator is handling the case, which the client is, the name of the case, where is the case located, the type of the case, what marketing stream it comes from, whether the case is a flat rate or an hourly, and possibly a short narrative field for recording essential notes about that particular case (important if that case is an outlier). That's just nine pieces of data to input into a simple spreadsheet.

Time Management

Obtain a small pocket calendar that breaks each day down in quarter hour increments. If you don't have a planner or a little pocket calendar, Day-timer is a great start. Just mark off blocks of time that are more than .25 as either B for billable, N for non-billable, A for administrative, O for ownership, M for marketing, or T for travel. Block off M for breakfast, lunch and dinner and G for goof-off time. Be honest with yourself. If you goof-off during working hours Monday through Friday, ask yourself why are you in business.

Keeping this record day in and day out over the first year that you're in business is well worth it. You capture your billable time and your marketing time and get to analyze how you are actually spending your time. Keep in mind you have to have X number of billable hours attributed to a particular week for you to stay in business.

With this method you can see:

- How much administrative time or non-billable time is you are engaged in to support the billable time?
- Are you doing your marketing? When are you attending to your ownership duties?
- Did you meet your goals? Did you exceed your goals? What is the total number of hours for the week related to your business?
- Is something getting in the way of you being able to do all the hours necessary to perform in your business? List those in your planner.

Peter Drucker said it best when he said, "that which gets measured, gets done." By managing your time, you'll find out that you get more things done.

Finding excuses for why you can't get things done will become glaringly evident in your time management log, and it's also going to be part of the answer as to why your bottom line isn't doing so well. Keep searching for ways to reduce your administrative and non-billable time during prime time. You will be able to expand the number of billable hours.

If you can grow these new time management habits, it will benefit you as you move forward. When you start working closely with associates or employees, the amount of your supervision and management time will go up and should be measured too.

For the time being, tackling your time management is the most critical day-to-day task that you can do. Attempt to make sure you are giving yourself enough time in the areas that are important such as billable time and marketing.

Budget

You should create a budget for the year you start so that you can compare your actuals against your business plan. How else will you know how well you're doing?

Making sure you have a budget set up for the following year, in either a paper fashion or in the accounting software, is a worthwhile exercise. How else do you keep score? How do you know how well you're doing? Of course, the final score is that you have money in your business checkbook week after week, month after month and that you don't have to dip into credit cards or a line of credit or a home equity loan. You're able to not only fund your living and business expenses, but you're also able to think in terms of growth because you don't have to take on additional debt to expand.

WHAT IS YOUR BUSINESS ENTITY GOING TO BE

SECTION NINE:
COUNTDOWN SUMMARY

BUILDING BLOCKS

Each section is to be worked in order. Once you have gone through all the exercises and checklists, you may be wondering, "How do I put this all together in my countdown from Day 90 to Day 0 and lift off?"

I recommend visiting the **Red Light / Green Light** checklist as you get a clearer picture of your business. If you are not having a "Hell, Yeah!" reaction to creating your business by this section, you should rethink your decision to spend time, effort, and money for your lift off.

If it's "Hell, Yeah!" then let's go.

Knowing your numbers is essential. It would be best if you nailed down your living expenses, business expenses (projected budget), and revenue projections. Know your weighted-average hourly rate so you can calculate your critical number. If these are foreign concepts at this stage of the book, I haven't done my job of explaining them to you.

Numbers first, because you are entering the **business** of Private Investigations. Otherwise, you will drift into thinking about this

SECTION NINE: COUNTDOWN SUMMARY

endeavor as a "paying hobby." There is nothing wrong with paying hobbies, but very rarely will they keep the lights on. When I was a solo working on Squire Investigations, I put in extra hours Monday through Thursday and Saturday morning, so that I could play with Hoda Genealogy all day Friday and Saturday afternoons. That time eventually morphed into Part-time, then Most-time, then Full-time as the money I was making with Hoda Genealogy surpassed my revenue from Squire Investigations. After one prominent case, I was able to fund the start-up of International Missing Heir Finders, LLC.

But I digress.

After you nail down the numbers needed to feed yourself, your family, and to pay Uncle Sam, we shift the focus to where it belongs: **The Customer.**

Why do you want to go into business and why is this important to you? My Why was to create a team of highly trained experts in insurance fraud investigation. My How was applying all my supervisory and managerial skills to my expertise in insurance fraud investigations. My What was investigations for the property and casualty insurance companies.

Most Private Investigators are the hammers always in search of a nail. The shift in thinking required is this: How does your Why align with customer needs? How does your How meet their needs with What services or products that you will provide? Are you open to learning new skill sets to meet more of your target audience's needs?

BUILDING BLOCKS

John planned to launch Independent Special Investigations from his Rolodex of contacts. These people already knew, liked, and trusted John from their previous experiences with him.

John had hired private investigators throughout the geographic area in which he wanted to compete. He knew who was where, and how much they charged.

As a start-up, John decided to price his offerings slightly below the market average to lure his contacts away from their present investigative solutions.

It worked. In less than four years, John had nine investigators working for him in New York, Massachusetts, Rhode Island, and Connecticut, with plans to move into New Jersey and Northern New England.

Tony's plan is to align his Why—the desire to work on his own out on the street again with no bureaucracy looking over his shoulder—directly to Professionals closer to his home by offering his What—high-end investigative skills and 27 years of contacts—with his How—scripted phone calls to set up face to face meetings with Attorneys, CPAs, Property Managers, and Financial Planners. His marketing and business plan looks very much like the example provided earlier in the marketing section.

SECTION NINE: COUNTDOWN SUMMARY

Beth's plan is more ambitious. Her personal expenses are low but having to replace all her life, and disability benefits in her business will be more expensive than for Tony, who has pension benefits, or John, whose wife's career provides all the benefits for the family.

Beth's business expenses are higher due to the IT costs of maintaining a website with e-commerce capability and a robust sales funnel.

Her Why is much like Tony in that, between the Army and working in the Armed Guard industry, she has chafed under the layers of management and is looking to be her own boss. Like John, she wants to train apprentices or newbies in her methods.

Beth's How is to attract inbound leads with an SEO-rich first page listing in the browser search results and to lead the customer through the sales funnel using e-Books, Free Reports, and Video Testimonials to get them to fill out the contact form. Beth consults with them via live chat, to qualify them, converts the sale by getting the assignment, getting them to fill out the retainer, and make payments through the website with a credit card or PayPal.

She, like Tony, will attend a Chamber of Commerce leads group, join Business Networks International (BNI). She will institute a referral program with high-end hair, beauty, nail and wellness salons. Her business cards will be displayed in independent coffee shops and area gyms.

She engages customers with her What, fairly-priced flat rates or budgets. She prices her surveillances in four-hour and eight-hour blocks.

Have you decided what your WHY, HOW and WHAT are?

Are you ready to Countdown? Say **Hell, Yeah!**

Day 90

- Decide on a Business Name and Type of Business. Secure Domain name.
- Secure your EIN number.

Day 89

- File for your LLC, S or C Corp., if you are not going to be a Sole Proprietorship.

Day 88

- Apply for your PI license *find out if your State has an exam requirement.
- Memorize the gun carry laws related to Private Investigators.

Day 87

- Open business bank account.
- Secure a business Credit Card.

Day 86

- Interview Accountants.
- Decide on your Accounting Software.
- Determine if you need to upgrade your computer and smartphone.

Day 85

- Immerse yourself in bookkeeping and accounting tutorials with your accounting software. (Rainy Saturdays are good for this exercise.)

SECTION NINE: COUNTDOWN SUMMARY

Day 84

- Move your expense and revenue numbers into a monthly budget in your accounting software. Create an annual Profit & Loss.

Day 83-82

- Begin planning your website build. Decide on DIY or get help. Be sure that your guru can't lock you out so you can refresh content.
- Engage a professional designer for your company logo. (List your job on Fiverr or Upwork.)

Day 82-81

- Decide on a web host server and website software

Day 80-79

- Rough out the website look and wiring (e.g., select your Wordpress theme)

Day 78-77

- Rough draft of Home Page and Services page content

Day 76-75

- Rough draft of About page, Contact Page, and FAQ content

Day 74-73

- Set up your e-Commerce plug-in and customize those templates.

Day 72-71

- Reach out for testimonials.

Day 70-69

- Create Grand Opening Newsletter

Day 68-60

- Create a FREE REPORT or e-Book for Target Audience.

Day 59-58

- Identify search terms with Google Keyword analytics.

Day 57-56

- Go over the content rough draft, adding in keywords without diluting the message.

Day 55

- Decide on Contact Page and Email Capture software.

Day 54-53

- Begin loading content on your website.

Day 52-51

- Add Auto Responders

Day 50

- Build Assignment Log

Day 49

- Test Accounting software for sending out invoices or from your Word Processing software email feature. Can your Software talk with your bank? Can you reconcile checking online?

Day 48

- Decide on a CRM method.

Day 47

- Play around with CRM tutorials. Create some fictitious customers.

SECTION NINE: COUNTDOWN SUMMARY

Day 46

- How are you going to track your time? Now is an excellent time to start.

Day 45-44

- Hire a designer to create business cards with your brand spanking new logo.

Day 43-40

- Hire a designer to create brochures, flyers, and sale promotions using your Logo.

Day 39

- Attend Chamber of Commerce leads groups and ask for advice on your design mock-ups. Point them to your website for additional suggestions.

Professionals are glad to offer advice over coffee but don't abuse or monopolize their time.

Day 38

- Introduce yourself to BNI. Float your Why, How, and What in your "Elevator Speech." A Private Investigator is always the coolest kid at the lunch table. Be professional and don't play to stereotype.

Getting to know business people before your launch date allows them to get to know, like, and begin trusting you, without the pressure of a sale.

Day 37

- Find out where your wildebeest (target audience) drinks. Don't be bashful. Go and observe.

Day 36-35

- Tweak your marketing copy on your website and in your collateral.

Day 34

- Check on business filings and licensing. Once your license has been granted, apply for the databases you need for your investigations.

Day 33

- Talk with your State Association about joining, the meetings schedule, and their preferred vendors for your Errors & Omission Coverage and your Surety Bond

Day 32

- Apply for your E&O and Surety Bond.

Day 31

- Meet with your final choice of accountants. Place upcoming milestones on your calendars. Run your budget by them. Does anything jump off the page at them? Come up with a realistic bail-out date, in case your revenues do not start to meet expenses and you hemorrhage cash at a dangerous rate.

Day 30

- Do you need letterhead and office supplies? Look for my stapler story at the end of this section. Plan your exit strategy from your present situation. How much notice do they require? If your banked personal days and vacation time is "Use it or Lose it," make sure not to leave any time on the table.

Day 29

- Decide on phone and fax capability. I have an old-fashion fax machine, and a dedicated line left over from the early days. Call me old-fashioned.

SECTION NINE: COUNTDOWN SUMMARY

Day 28

- Offer complimentary assignments to key influencers in exchange for testimonials and to test your processes.

Day 27

- Start marketing for a soft launch. Begin populating your CRM with soft targets. Practice listening to clarify their needs.

Day 26

- Begin daily practice on your outbound phone call scripts with soft targets. Put these activities in your schedule now and build your habit, before it matters.

Day 25-21

- Meet with prospects following the AIDA process.

Day 20

- Sit with your supporters and go over what you have done and what still needs to be done.

Day 19

- Find conferences or seminars to attend that will provide an opportunity to sharpen your investigative and marketing skills. Make sure those expenses are in your budget.

Day 18-10

- Prioritize all remaining tasks. What's not done needs to get cleaned up here. If you are on target, continue to market, but now for paying clients.

Day 9-8

- Return to Chamber of Commerce leads groups or BNI meetings. Renew contacts and make new friends. Showing up is half the battle.

Day 7- 1

- You are a short-timer at work now. Let as many people know at work or in your work sphere that next week, you will be in business for yourself. Do not tread on non-competes. Respect everybody and don't burn bridges. On nights and weekends, market and work on any soft launch assignments.

Day Zero

- Liftoff!

Congratulations! Look at what you have done to prepare yourself for this day. It all started when you said, **"Hell, Yeah!"**

SECTION NINE: COUNTDOWN SUMMARY

My Stapler Story

Back in 1997, I was getting ready to leave a significant corporation and go out on my own. We were just at the dawn of the Internet and Email was still something new (with an AOL account). I was in my company's supply closet, drooling at all the supplies in there. Everything I needed for my desk at my new office at home was in arm's reach. I made my list of what I needed instead and went to Staples.

Back then, we stapled our invoices to paper reports and folded them to fit in a printed envelope. Yes, I even licked the stamp and walked the finished product out to the mailbox. Email is so much easier and faster.

At Staples, I bought a **Swingline Stapler** that I still have on my desk today, twenty-plus years later and a box of 5,000 staples. They weren't expensive at all, but I paused for a minute and thought about it before I put it into my basket. If I went through that whole box of staples, I would be stapling tons of invoices to tons of reports. Hell, if I went through that entire box, I was darn sure I'd be still in business.

Sometime in December of 2008, my accountant was going over my books and reached for the trusty Swingline. It was empty. I went to the supply drawer, and that box of 5,000 staples was empty. I told my accountant the story. We laughed. It was a good day.

He then used a paper clip.

Tony has come a long way from wondering what it would feel like to retire from the only real job he ever had. As much as he cursed the suffocating stratification of the NYPD, it was comforting to know a paycheck arrived magically in his checking account every month. Those benefits he took for granted have a real price tag on them now. He is learning how to budget his personal expenses. He learned how to build a business budget in the software his accountant recommended. Every once in a while, he visits his website to see his company's name, logo, and his photo. When he mentions that he will pull the pin, people begin asking him for his business card. Even better, he starts gathering contact information in his simple CRM.

Little steps taken in order, one step at a time, work for him. He gets a handle on his numbers and figures out who his target audience is, and he focuses his message in a way that doesn't sound salesy or scammy. He can look at the professional sitting across his desk in the eye and not blink when the subject of price comes up. Some cop skills are transferable!

Each step in his journey is the next logical step on his path. He is excited to leave the comfort of the lagoon and start swimming in the ocean surf.

SECTION NINE: COUNTDOWN SUMMARY

Beth is working extra hours on her job while she bootstraps her company. She cherry-picks an employee from the guard service to train. They work together during the soft launch and are a good fit. The website works; all the buttons and links do what they are supposed to do. The Free Reports attract email sign-ups, and a six-email autoresponder sequence moves the prospect further into the sales funnel. The live chat function gives her immediate access to leads, and she qualifies them on the spot. She learns to separate the tire-kickers from the motivated buyers very quickly. She directs them to the contact page, the terms of agreement button, and the shopping cart.

Yes, Beth Clark has a shopping cart for her business and almost all the buyers want her Open Source Intelligence (OSINT) special. What they learn about the subject of the investigation is well worth the up-sell to them, and it was painless to add, as Beth found out after the first couple of nervous asks.

People are buying what she has to offer. She receives interest in her referral program, and she does a few freebies for hair stylists who thought their lovers might be stepping out on them while they were cutting and coloring.

She and her employee provide excellent service. Testimonials are abundant, and Beth has already added compelling videos to the website. All of this while she is part-time. Of course, she's working long hours, six or seven days a week, but it's time invested in the goal, and the light is there at the end of the tunnel. She is her own boss and loving it. Looking at the numbers, she thinks both she and her employee can go full time sooner rather than later.

SECTION TEN: BONUS STORY

AN ANECDOTE

I will never forget the time or date. There I was on a rainy Friday afternoon, September 21, 2012, approximately 2:31 PM. It was the last day of summer, and I had just received an attachment in an email on a significant case. It came in while I was talking with my senior Certified Genealogist, Claire.

Sure enough, the information contained in that attachment blindsided us. The story behind it is for another day; however, suffice it to say the news was disastrous.

I had started International Missing Heir Finders, the missing heir research and forensic genealogy firm, seven years earlier.

Primarily how the business worked was this: I would find estates in Probate where people died without a will and where, in a small handful of those cases, not all heirs were accounted for. I would use Forensic Genealogy to find who they were and my Private Investigation skills to locate them. I made a simple pitch. I told them they were heirs to an estate. For a percentage of their inheritance, I would tell them where it was and would hire an attorney to get their money for them. The heirs would not have to front me a dime or pay expenses. I would get paid when they got paid. If they got nothing, they would owe me nothing and would not have to pay any expenses. High Stakes. High risk, and high reward.

Earlier that year, I had elected to close down the business slowly. This case, along with a handful of others, was meant to carry me through 2013 and into 2014.

I had been sitting in a co-working space and stumbled out to my wife's car. She asked me what was wrong. I explained the situation to her. This sad news just drove home the point to her that I'd been engaged in a high-stakes, high-risk, high-reward business and here she was, again, hearing what appeared to be seriously bad news.

I had trouble sleeping that night, and at about three o'clock in the morning I trudged downstairs to my home office desk and started going over the research again. I realized the information I had received in that email was severe, but not fatal to the overall case. On Monday morning, we would embark on the way to salvage the case, which we eventually did, two years later but, after paying off our extensive legal bills, only received about a tenth of what we should have.

Through that summer in 2012, I had undertaken a couple of proofs of concepts to see if there was viability to ideas I had on a couple of online B2B specialty niches. Within six weeks of each proof, I realized performing the proofs of concept saved me from expending a lot of capital and time in determining whether or not there would be customers for those business models.

Unfortunately, the bad news late that Friday afternoon meant the money I was to receive from that case, which was earmarked for paying down the business credit line, funding my salary for 2013, and paying for my daughter's advanced degree had evaporated into the rainy mist.

Now, over the first sun-splashed fall weekend of 2012, the decision had to be made—quickly—on how to return to profitability.

I had kept a handful of private investigative clients over the years from 2005 through 2012 and looked to them as the rebirth of my private investigation business. However, first, I had to get a handle on my expenses. The missing heir research business had been very profitable for me, and it allowed me to place more emphasis on revenue. Somehow, a fat checkbook took the pressure off of me to keep a sharp eye on all my expenses.

For the next three weeks, I slowly reviewed my credit card statements for the past three years, along with my personal and business checkbook registers.

I was shocked by what I found. The amount of fat in my expenses was eye-popping. I saw that the I was paying for monthly charges for internet radio on cars we no longer owned. We had gym memberships to gyms we no longer attended. There were duplicate bills or other expenses for which there were no explanations. I saw how much money I was spending at Dunkin' Donuts and Starbucks every month. I saw how much I was paying for lunches and how much we were spending going out to eat. Needless to say, during those seven years, we took more vacations and spent more money on those vacations as a percentage of our total expenses. Vacation costs had crept up on us over the years.

It was the first time we sat down and analyzed our personal budget since I first started my business in September 1997. My review of bank statements and credit card statements had eroded as the company grew and became more profitable.

SECTION TEN: BONUS STORY

It was a real eye-opener to see how much money we were spending.

Before launching a new business on January 1 of 2013, the first matter of business was to get a handle on our personal expenses—similar to what you have been asked to do in this book.

Next, I determined what the business expenses were, and what business expenses would remain or change for 2013. A careful review of the budget and actual expenses for several years gave a clear indication, again, where I had taken on extra costs that were no longer needed. I was still paying a monthly subscription fee for databases we no longer used. I ended those quickly.

From a revenue standpoint, I had a look at every one of the remaining missing heir research cases and determined high, medium, and low payout probabilities. I placed them on a spreadsheet to gauge the earliest and latest times these cases might pay out. Having had several years of tracking these numbers allowed me to estimate a reasonable schedule of how much the handful of cases would pay out and when.

This bought me some time. I also realized I did not have to hit the ground on January first earning a full replacement income. The monies I would gradually earn during 2013 could be supplemented by the occasional missing heir research case payment.

When I saw my actual living expenses and business expenses, I understood the urgency to create a new business. I looked to build a scaled-down, solo PI business and mapped out the timeframe by which I had to reach sustainability.

Years earlier, a good friend and former employee, Jon Sitek, had shared the idea of naming a company Elm City Detectives. In Connecticut, many towns have nicknames. Bridgeport is Park City, Danbury is Hat City, Waterbury is Brass City, and Hartford is Insurance City. New Haven was known as Elm City. I thought about how I wanted to go about this business, and what this business meant with the end in mind. What was I going to do with this business? Where was I going to go for customers? How was I going to attract these customers?

I had concerns about returning to high-level private investigations again, as I had to invest most of my time and energy from 2005 to 2012 into forensic genealogy and the investigative skills associated with it.

I'd worked up a few criminal defense cases in the intervening years, and handled some cases where the locating people were of the utmost importance to my still existing clientele. Since my expertise in location services was part of my missing heir research work, it was easy to extend those skill sets to all lawyers who had to locate parties to their cases before going to trial.

However, it was validation from a group of private investigators I'd known for years, through my time as a Regional Director for the National Association of Legal Investigators, that finally prompted me to jump back into the game. They had no problem telling me I could blow the rust off my old skill sets and very quickly get back on my feet. That validation was important to me because I was concerned that if I were to return to this business again, I would not be able to work at the same high level as I had done previously. This would be a source of high stress for me.

So from early October through Christmas of 2012, things began to fall into place rather quickly. Starting with the end in mind, I decided I would start up Elm City Detectives as a sole proprietorship until my retirement date, which had now been pushed back because of the evaporation of that significant case, as well as losing the opportunity to sell International Missing Heir Finders to my employees.

Elm City Detectives would stay in business until my retirement date. At that time, I would give my clients sixty days' notice and then would work off the remaining cases in that period. I would turn off the proverbial lights and lock the door behind me.

This was to be a lifestyle business. I would work directly for attorneys in the greater New Haven area, mostly in criminal defense investigation and personal injury investigation. I still had one or two clients from the insurance defense days, and the transferable skill sets were still there. I remained interested in working to obtain proof of reasonable doubt for criminal defense attorneys, as well as working personal injury cases for attorneys with clients who needed to find the evidence that the other party was indeed at fault.

I dissolved the LLC for International Missing Heir Finders and created a sole proprietorship for Elm City Detectives. I created two new business checking and savings accounts at the bank under Elm City Detectives, as well as a new credit card. Elm City Detectives would officially start January 1st and monies coming in from the Missing Heir Research cases would flow into that checkbook. A new QuickBooks account was set up, and a new budget was created for 2013.

With the Fall colors on display over the New Haven Town Green in mid-October, I sat down in the Chamber of Commerce offices overlooking the Green, as I had done in previous years, and worked on my marketing plan. I had a clear understanding of my target audience, who they were, and how I was going to market to them. I used the iThoughts HD app for my marketing genogram and created a Google spreadsheet for my assignment log. I would keep a separate list of prospects and customers in an Excel spreadsheet.

I planned to send out a quarterly newsletter to both prospects and clientele with special announcements, news releases, and seasonal specials.

I registered the domain name for Elm City Detectives and built a WordPress website. The Home page, About page, Services page, and FAQ page were created in rapid succession. I gathered testimonials while also trying to expand my customer reach by contacting customers I had before 2005, and ones that I retained over the eight years.

On November 12, 2012, I was contacted by a criminal defense attorney working on an appellate case for a young man who had been in jail for six years on a murder he didn't commit. I had worked on the co-defendant's, and in May 2008, the codefendant was acquitted.

Just before that trial, this young man's attorney at the time pled him guilty to 38 years in jail for the homicide he didn't commit. Since I understood the underlying case, I was the logical choice to work on this young man's appellate case.

In December 2012, I was anxious about the launch of Elm City Detectives and how it would be received. I attended a Christmas party hosted by a law firm that I had stayed friendly with. That evening, one of their attorneys threw his arm around my shoulder and told many of his friends to utilize my services. He went out of his way to extol some of the more creative ways I uncovered the facts for him. He told them about some of the cases I'd worked on and what the results meant to his bottom line.

That evening I picked up a dozen business cards and, the next morning, titled the header of one of my genogram marketing streams with the name of his law firm + Holiday party. I entered those twelve lawyers' names as having received glowing testimonials and referrals underneath that law firm's family tree.

Several months later, during a business lunch, that same attorney turned me on two additional law firms doing work in New Haven, and one of those law firms became one of my largest customers.

In the beginning, my marketing plan included contacting lawyers in the Greater New Haven area. These were my target audience. I scheduled appointments to meet with them and talk about how I could upgrade their investigative solutions.

With a leaner personal budget and a leaner business budget for 2013, the push to my critical number could be gradual. Within a short period, I reached the required number of weekly billable hours to break even, and make a profit that year using the steps outlined in this book.

I made five calls a day, Monday through Thursday, for an hour. I received callbacks on four of those five phone calls, and during that callback, I followed my scripts which allowed me to qualify the prospect.

Two of those four callbacks agreed to meet me for a 15-minute appointment before morning court.

Of those two law firms that I met with and made a presentation to, one would proceed to hire me and provide assignments within 60 days. The other one, although they were happy with their present PI and did not to hire me immediately, with persistent follow-up over the years, eventually came into the fold.

Gradually, I moved many prospects onto my customer spreadsheet. I sent out press releases on our headline cases from the New Haven Register and the Connecticut Post, the Bridgeport paper.

I tracked everything.

At some point, I retired my Massachusetts and New York State private investigators licenses and concentrated only on the clientele in Connecticut.

I realized that lawyers outside of the Greater New Haven radius were reticent to utilize my services, thinking that I only handled assignments in the Greater New Haven area. Reasonable, given that Elm City Detectives is nicknamed after New Haven, so I went through a rebranding exercise and changed the name of the company to Hoda investigations, LLC. I gave the limited liability company the tagline Serving Connecticut Trial Attorneys Since 1997. This clearly expressed that I worked all over Connecticut for trial attorneys, whether they be personal injury, criminal defense, insurance defense, or divorce attorneys.

I instituted flat rates. I noticed that over the course of several years, I received repetitive assignments from many of my customers, requiring the same skill sets. By logically completing those tasks and utilizing best practices, I was able to determine how much time and expense they would take. I crafted my flat rates to be profitable for me while assuring the client there would be no additional cost and no "stair stepping" of their expenses.

I also instituted what I called the CashFlow Snapshot, which allowed me to see the status of the company with a glance on the 15th and the 30th of every month.

I started with my operating account checkbook balance and subtract out my outstanding checks, that tells me how much money is available in there. I look at my budget for the month and see what one-time-only expenses are coming up, and the average costs that I will incur. I subtract them from my net checkbook balance. Sales tax and monthly tax withholdings are next, and they are moved to the tax account.

How much I could take as an owner's draw was dependent on how low I could bring the checkbook, what my monthly draw was, and how much in receivables I had coming in. I manually count the invoices in the closed and unpaid cases to see how much is coming in. If receivables were low, then I kept more in checking as a cushion. Remember the adage "Cash is King."

I can tell you there was no magic in this build out. It was incremental, based upon executing a marketing plan, keeping track of the numbers, and watching my metrics to make sure I was doing what I said I was going to do. Over half of my work now

SECTION TEN: BONUS STORY

comes from attorneys outside of the Greater New Haven area, and I made inroads into other practice areas where my skill sets matched up very nicely with their practices.

I can tell you "90 days to lift off" is possible. I did a massive pivot from early October of 2012 to New Years of 2013.

When you decide you want to go out on your own as a private investigator follow the steps outlined herein. Don't skip any of the exercises. Take the time to make sure of your numbers. Check them twice.

You really should get buy-in from your loved ones, close family members and friends. They should be there to support you during this time.

Get your financial house in order. Make sure you understand what your expenses are.

Determine how much revenue you have to make to replace the loss of income from your job and to cover your taxes.

What is your Critical Number?

Does your one-page business plan and one-page marketing plan make sense?

Make sure you have the plans in place before you offer your two weeks' notice or change careers.

Go back to the Introduction and ask yourself the **Red Light/ Green Light** questions one more time. Give yourself the time to get your business running, but have a bail-out date on the calendar at which point you will call it a day if you are hemorrhaging cash.

As an old homicide detective once said, "There ain't nothing to it, but to do it."

I believe this book offers you the opportunity to use your energy and enthusiasm to overcome all obstacles, to find out what your true North is and to follow your roadmap to success.

I thank you for staying with me to the end.

I hope I've earned your time and your trust.

Now go out and do it.

*To my father John J. Hoda
for teaching me how to work hard, be generous,
and how to provide for your family.*

NEED MORE HELP?

If you are launching your business soon and have questions or you are having trouble getting your company off the ground, I am available for a FREE 30-minute consultation. Please go to the contact form at www.ThePICoach.com and schedule a phone call with me. It may be an easy fix.

Also

I only coach PIs and limit my time to just eight individual sessions a week so that I can concentrate on helping each client reach their goals and achieve a life/work balance. My personal experience with coaches has been fantastic. One coach helped me save my business and every time I utilized the services of a coach, the cost of their advice was paid back within months.

ABOUT JOHN A. HODA, CLI, CFE

John A. Hoda is a licensed private investigator, blogger, and podcaster. He coaches other PIs how to be successful at **ThePICoach.com**

He graduated in 1975 with a B.S. in Criminology from Indiana University of Pennsylvania.

He is a former police officer, insurance fraud investigator, and has run several PI businesses over three decades.

He has written numerous articles for PI Magazine and is the creator of the DVD: *The Ultimate Guide to Taking Statements*. His cases have headlined in the Philadelphia Inquirer and the New Haven Register. He sat on the board of the National Association of Legal Investigators and the CT Assoc of Licensed Private Investigators. He is a Certified Legal Investigator and a Certified Fraud Examiner.

SECTION TEN: BONUS STORY

John also writes fiction and has been a lifetime athlete playing club soccer and playing/coaching semi-professional football.

His podcast audience at My Favorite Detective Stories is growing every day. John interviews past and present investigators about their specialties and teases out what it takes to make for a successful investigation. The entire podcast catalog can be found at **JohnHoda.com**

OTHER BOOKS BY JOHN A. HODA

Get your FREE *Mugshots: My Favorite Detective Stories* downloaded in your favorite format right to your inbox by going to- **JohnHoda.com.**

Come ride around the country with veteran investigator John A. Hoda as he searches for the truth. He has selected great stories from a forty-plus year career and keeps serving them up like free refills at the all-night diner.

Non-Fiction

How to Market Your Private Investigation Business: Less Than 5 Hours a Week. Really!

How to Boost Your Private Investigation Business: Make $1,000 every Working Day!

How to Rocket Your Private Investigation Business: The Complete Series

SECTION TEN: BONUS STORY

Fiction

Odessa on the Delaware: Introducing Marsha O'Shea

A Crime Thriller with a mystery twist set in Philadelphia pitting a Russian mob enforcer against a homeless Marine Corp veteran. FBI Agent Marsha O'Shea is drawn into the case with a secret pushing her to follow the clues, only to uncover a greater secret that may get her killed in the final showdown.

Phantasy Baseball: It's About A Second Chance.

A thirty-nine-year-old little league coach discovers he has a magical pitch and gets a one in a million chance to try out for his beloved Philadelphia Phillies. He is unprepared for the roller-coaster magic-carpet ride in the Big Leagues.

ACKNOWLEDGMENTS

Rekka Jay for Cover Design, Illustrations, Editing, Formatting, Layout, Patience and Forgiveness.

Joanna Penn of **TheCreativePenn.com** for the information and inspiration needed to tackle my first non-fiction project.

My advanced copy readers who saved my butt countless times: Luis Reyes, Ron Getner, Rich Robertson, Brandon Perron, Cynthia Hetherington, Brian Ritucci, Jayne McElfresh, Lisa Garcia, Kate Minchin, Burt Hodge, Tony Raymond, Paul Rubin

The **Written Word-Milford Writers Group** for their support and encouragement.

Thanks to all.

www.ingramcontent.com/pod-product-compliance
Lightning Source LLC
Chambersburg PA
CBHW030442300426
44112CB00009B/1131